Game of two halves

Football Yesterday & Today

First published in 2003
10 9 8 7 6 5 4 3 2 1

This edition published for Index Books Ltd 2004

A CIP catalogue record for this book is available from the British Library.

ISBN 1-86200-160-X

Managing Editor: Nigel Matheson
Design & Project Art Direction: Darren Jordan
Production: Lisa French
Printed in Singapore

Game of two halves

Football Yesterday & Today

TIM GLYNNE-JONES

INDEX

Contents

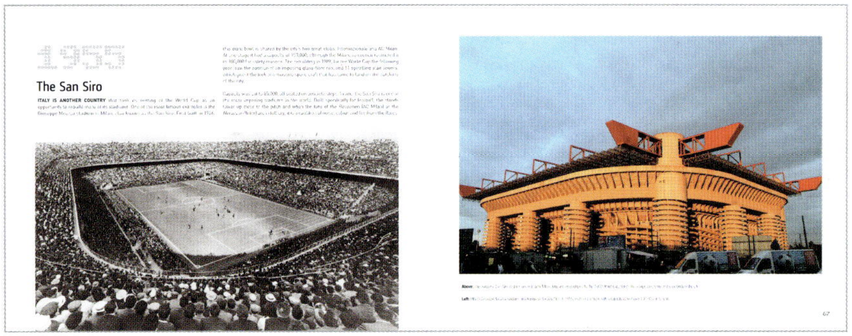

1957
Authority figure

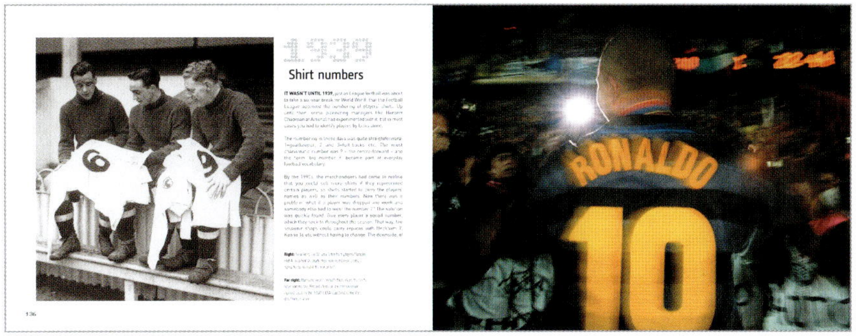
1939
Shirt numbers
RONALDO
10

1966
Yeeeeeeeees!

Foreword

I'VE FOUND IT ABSOLUTELY FASCINATING to delve back in time with these football photographs jogging my memory. Even my wife, Barbara, who never liked football has sat with me, marvelling at how things have changed. Barbara had the good sense to marry me more than forty years ago, and she recalls the kit we used to wear, the heavy footballs and the way the crowds behaved. I only wish me Dad was still alive to see football nowadays, to sit in comfort and see more grass on the pitch than he ever saw in his days in Middlesborough. He'd have loved this book.

That photo of Alex James and his baggy shorts! Hell's fire, my hand-me-down long trousers were higher up my ankles than those shorts! How did James ever run around the pitch? And what a warm, lovely photo of the supporters passing that boy down to the front, so he wouldn't get crushed. That's what happened in my time as a player in the fifties and sixties as well. Nobody fell out with anyone in the crowd, we players could hear the banter, but I don't recall any obscene chanting. We were all too happy to be out in the fresh air, up in the North-East. The men would work in the factories on Saturday morning, pick up their bairns and take them to the match. That was the highlight of the week and the players knew their responsibilities to the area. Football was a genuine working-class pleasure, there was little else to do. No wonder we had big families, we had to make our own entertainment.

The photo of the players smoking in the bath after the game struck a chord with me. At Middlesbrough, we had a player called Bill Harris, a Welsh international who smoked like a chimney. I never went near him off the pitch, because I'd get a lungful of smoke and ash all over me. In a small, communal bath, with three players to a wall, Bill Harris was given a lot of space as he puffed away!

The reactions of the players to scoring goals has changed drastically in my time. We'd have a handshake, perhaps a ruffle of the hair and that was it. No kissing or taking off the shirt and waving it around. I couldn't even get a girl to kiss me, never mind my team-mates when I'd scored but I do understand the emotion of scoring a goal. I did that a few times, you know. I think it's OK to have a kiss, but save me all that shirt-waving, especially when there's a vest underneath!

But, you know, one thing hasn't changed down the years in football. It only takes a second to score a goal. No matter how many passes are involved, how heavy the pitch or the ball. It remains a simple game – only the players and the daft chairmen complicate it. This book is compiled with love to celebrate the greatest game. My 14-year-old grandson, Stephen is a fanatic for the game. He knows all the statistics and who was bought from where. Well, after I make him read this book, he'll be better informed about how football has evolved down the years. If I could afford to buy a coffee table, I'd even buy one to stick this book on it....

December 22, 1958: Brian Clough runs out on to the pitch during his days as a player for Sunderland. He also played for Middlesbrough and England

September 19, 1999: Cloughie makes an emotional return to his beloved City ground, the place where he once walked on water, to watch Forest take on Wolves

One:

Stars of the show

Right: January 21, 1939: Chelsea and Fulham players indulge in a bit of action at Stamford Bridge which has Spot the Ball editors all over the country in a lather

1932

Training exercises

ONE OF THE MAJOR DIFFERENCES between the footballers of yesterday and today is their level of fitness. Training methods have evolved and improved since the game began, but the last two decades of the 20th century saw the most radical changes of all in British football.

Up until then, the 'British style' of play, which relied heavily on physical strength and not so heavily on ball skills, had managed to hold its own fairly well on the international stage. But by the late 1980s, it was deemed to be falling behind the rest of Europe, a situation made worse by the exclusion of English clubs from European competitions as a result of fatal crowd trouble involving Liverpool fans at Heysel Stadium.

Training shifted in emphasis away from brute force; there was more ball work and exercises designed for agility. As foreign coaches entered the British game, they brought in the radical concept of training not just in the morning, as had been the norm, but in the afternoon too. There is still work to do to improve the technique of the British footballer, but progress is being made. Whether the modern player can jump as high as these Chelsea players of the 1930s, however, is open to debate.

Above: Training in Britain has become more ball-oriented. Here the England World Cup squad practise in Saitama before their group opener against Sweden in June, 2002

Left: Chelsea obviously expect a lot of aerial bombardment from Liverpool in their forthcoming FA Cup tie in February, 1932, as (l–r) Barber, O'Dowd, Law, Cheyne and Pearson get in some jumping practice

1952

Physique

LOOKING BACK AT OLD FOOTAGE of professional football, there appears to be a marked difference in the athleticism of the players of yesteryear, compared to their modern counterparts. This could be down to one of three things: the jerky black and white film makes the players' movement look much less fluid and graceful, the kit they wore was less than flattering to the athletic frame or they weren't very athletic in those days. This third option is hard to believe. After all, these were the elite players of their day and therefore far more athletic than the average man in the street. Can mankind really have evolved so far in so short a time?

Much more plausible is explanation two. Just look at Arsenal's Alex James. One of the star players of his day, he looks like he's just done a hard shift at the coalface. The boots are huge, the shirt is loose and baggy, with a wing collar that ought to require a pilot's licence, and the shorts are simply enormous. Pulled up too high and hanging down too low, they would have used three times as much material as the shorts modelled by the svelte Ruud Gullit in the 1980s.

Left: Alex James, one of the Arsenal stars of the 1950s, cuts a dashing figure in his wing-collared shirt, knee-length shorts and enormous boots

Right: Ruud Gullit, the consummate athletic footballer of the 1980s and 1990s, captures the limelight in his AC Milan kit against Spanish side Real Madrid

1978

Training run

OH TO BE A PROFESSIONAL FOOTBALLER! That's the life: the money, the fame, the adulation, the gruelling training runs... Oh yes, you don't get handsomely rewarded for playing the game you love without being prepared to sweat. Training methods have changed in so many ways over the years, but nobody has yet found an alternative to the long-distance run as a means of building up stamina and testing the players' resolve. "Attitude training," Brian Clough used to call it.

Players hate it. After all, what is running when there's no ball? It's a traditional part of pre-season preparation, when there's nothing to be done with all that close-season flab but to run it off.

In the 1960s, members of Bill Nicholson's great Spurs side turned the training run to their advantage. Once out of sight of the manager, they would take a diversion to the local pub, down a couple of pints, then rejoin the run for the finishing leg. These days players aren't permitted out of the training ground, partly for their own safety, but partly, no doubt, thanks to the exploits of those cheeky Spurs players.

Above: Members of the Chinese team, Shenghua, carve a trail through the snow as they train at the Kunming camp in January, 2000

Left: Even the supremely gifted have to put in the leg work. Brazil's legendary team of 1970, with Pele third from the left, get in some stamina work for the World Cup

1955

Team photo

WHOEVER THE PHOTOGRAPHER was who first arranged two rows of players, one in front of the other – those at the back standing, those at the front crouching or sitting – established a format that has lasted unchallenged for more than a century. Ask any group of players to line up for the team photo and they will instinctively arrange themselves into this formation, the tallest at the back, the shortest at the front.

Okay, so there's an indisputable logic to it, but what other art form bows to logic for so many years? Where is the avant-garde lensman to challenge the order of things, to position his subjects in four groups, one in each corner of the frame, for example?

The team of African kids are from the Andy Cole Children's Foundation in Zimbabwe, set up by the former Manchester United forward. Their Vodafone-sponsored shirts may form an amusing juxtaposition with the state of the pitch and the makeshift goal behind them, but when it comes to the team photo, they all know the drill – just as the shivering players of Huddersfield Town did in 1955.

Above: October 1, 2001: kids at the Andy Cole Children's Foundation in Zimbabwe pose for a team photo wearing the colours of Cole's cub at the time, Manchester United

Left: Never mind the snow, the photographer's here and the shot has to be taken. The Huddersfield Town team line up uncomplainingly before a game on February 2, 1955

Get 'em young

KIDS ARE THE FUTURE of the game, everybody knows that. Matt Busby spotted it when he took over at Manchester United and created the famous Busby Babes. In the 1980s, Alex Ferguson rekindled the youth system at Old Trafford and achieved even greater success. Today, every club knows the value of securing the stars of the future at an early age.

In fact, it's become something of an obsession, with clubs conducting cloak and dagger operations to 'steal' promising youngsters from under the noses of their rivals. There are rules designed to prevent clubs offering inducements to parents to ensure that, when the time comes, their kid signs on the dotted line for them and not the club up the road. These rules are broken all the time but it's almost impossible to prove.

But while Busby and Ferguson, up to a point, put the emphasis on local youngsters, today the net is spread far wider. Areas of developing talent have been identified around the world and academies set up, partly to help the underprivileged kids to make the most of themselves, but also to establish a new source of talent for the club back in Britain.

Left: An England international at football and cricket, Denis Compton congratulates Acton and Chiswick schoolboys on winning the Compton Trophy in 1952

Right: Manchester United star Ryan Giggs, still only 19 himself, performs for children in Soweto on a club tour of South Africa in July, 1993

32

The football family

WE CANNOT TALK ABOUT THE CONTRASTS in football yesterday and today without mentioning attitudes to race. It is a delicate subject and one that, in an ideal world, wouldn't merit a mention, but these photographs highlight perfectly one of the most fundamental changes to the game's soul. The players in Arsenal's all-conquering team of the 1930s were all white. The Arsenal side that won the Double in 2002 was predominantly black. That is not to say that black players have become the dominant force in football – the Manchester United side that swept all before them in the 1990s was mainly white – but what it shows is that the balance has evened up.

As recently as the 1980s, black players had to fight against racial prejudice on a regular basis in order to fulfil their footballing ambitions and it was rare to see more than one or two black players in any side. The rapid development of the game in Africa has increased the resources of black talent and, critically, clubs and managers have been open-minded about signing them. Twenty years ago, that would not have always have been the case.

Right: Arsenal stars (left to right) Frank Moss, Eddie Hapgood and Cliff Bastin in 1934 during a decade of Arsenal dominance in which they won the Championship five times

Far right: Left to right: Ashley Cole, Patrick Vieira and Sol Campbell celebrate winning the Premiership title for Arsenal after a 1–0 win over rivals Manchester United at Old Trafford in May, 2002

SEGA
SEGA
23

1971

Genius

AH, GENIUS. THAT ELUSIVE QUALITY, that mercurial prize that all managers dream of but few wake up to find. In British football, with its emphasis on work-rate, power and pace, the appreciation of genius is a complex thing.

We love that diamond in the rough, but can we trust it? After all, genius is not reliable or consistent and it's certainly not forever. We ache to embrace genius as it emerges but our desire to keep it, to preserve it, to demand of it, only hastens its demise.

But still the footballing genius can leave a bigger impression in a few short years than the stalwart who ploughs his honest furrow from teenage to late-30s. It is more than just being a great player; it is the ability to surprise, to lift us out of our seats. And the genius deserves our respect because you can guarantee that throughout his development he has been encouraged to change his ways, to play for the team, to work on the things he can't do, rather than honing his ability to dance round four defenders and chip the keeper from impossible angles. Is genius alone enough to make a player great? The truth is in the eye of the beholder.

Left: Even Ron Harris can't stop George Best getting his shot away as the Irish genius pulls the strings for Manchester United against Chelsea in 1971

Right: In one of his finest games for England, Paul Gascoigne drives past Ruud Gullit and Frank Rijkaard of Holland in a 0–0 draw at the 1990 World Cup

The hero

THE GAME IS FULL OF STARS, but there are precious few heroes. To be a hero takes more than just ability, it takes endurance, determination, passion and desire – all the attributes that fans display constantly but all too seldom see from their teams. Heroism comes from glory earned in adversity, when you've fought the odds and come through. Heroes have broad shoulders, they take responsibility, they are leaders of men.

In the 1950s the Welsh colossus, John Charles, became a hero for Juventus fans. He remains to this day one of the few British players to have achieved success on the Continent and is remembered with great fondness by the people of Turin.

David Beckham became a hero for England in 2001 when he scored a spectacular free-kick against Greece to send his country to the World Cup. It wasn't just the goal, but the relentless determination of his whole performance that earned him such admiration. He was already a hero for Manchester United fans, of course, who knew well that his flamboyant public profile was underpinned by a solid commitment to the cause.

There can be no greater honour for a player than to be carried shoulder-high by the fans. It is evidence that, despite the huge gulf in wealth and status, you are regarded as one of them.

Above: April 14, 1999, and David Beckham is carried by fans from the Villa Park pitch after setting Manchester United on their way to a famous FA Cup semi-final win over Arsenal

Left: John Charles, one of the few British players to succeed in Italian football, gets the hero treatment after leading Juventus to Italian Cup triumph in 1958

Star signing

THE BUYING AND SELLING OF PLAYERS has always been one of the most intriguing aspects of the professional game. It's even inspired countless 'fantasy manager' games for fans to play, based on the business of buying the best players you can without blowing your budget. It's a skill that most football managers still struggle with today.

New signings have the potential to excite and amaze the fans, whether it's the controversial switch of a big name player to a rival club, such as Eric Cantona's move from Leeds to Manchester United, or the astute purchase of an unknown who will go on to be a star, such as Kevin Keegan joining Liverpool from Scunthorpe.

In latter years, clubs have cottoned on to the fervour generated by such signings and have made a major drama out of the signing ceremony. These pictures draw an amusing comparison between two Chelsea signings, 61 years apart, and the relative amount of attention they attracted. The somewhat furtive handshake extended to Cecil Allen couldn't be in more marked contrast to the lights and cameras surrounding Gianfranco Zola. Such hype, of course, can weigh heavily on the shoulders of the transferred player, although in Zola's case he was well able to carry the burden.

Right: November 19, 1935, and Irish international Cecil Allen (left) is given a low-key welcome to Chelsea by fellow countryman Bambrick

Far right: The unveiling of new signing Gianfranco Zola at Stamford Bridge attracts massive attention from press, television and radio in a media call of November, 1996

UMBRO
Coors

Icons

THE CONCEPT OF FOOTBALLER AS ICON really took off in the 1960s. Until then, only a handful of players had been deemed sufficiently high-profile for companies to use them to market their goods. But with the likes of George Best assuming pop-star status, and then England winning the World Cup, captained by the dashing Bobby Moore, footballers suddenly came into vogue.

Even so, the deals they were offered were a world apart from the multi-million-pound sponsorship contracts enjoyed by today's football icons, such as Alessandro del Piero. Aside from the money, what football agent today would allow his player to be photographed without his trousers? This rather bizarre portrait of the England captain wearing just his shirt and socks and holding his jacket is fairly typical of the awkward photo shoots to which the 1960s stars merrily subjected themselves. But any opportunity to be 'got up' in posh clothes was welcomed with open arms.

Today, rather than being made to look merely respectable, footballers expect to be turned into gods, or superbeings. Image is everything, and at every photo shoot there'll be an army of agents, stylists and advisers clamouring to ensure that the trousers stay on.

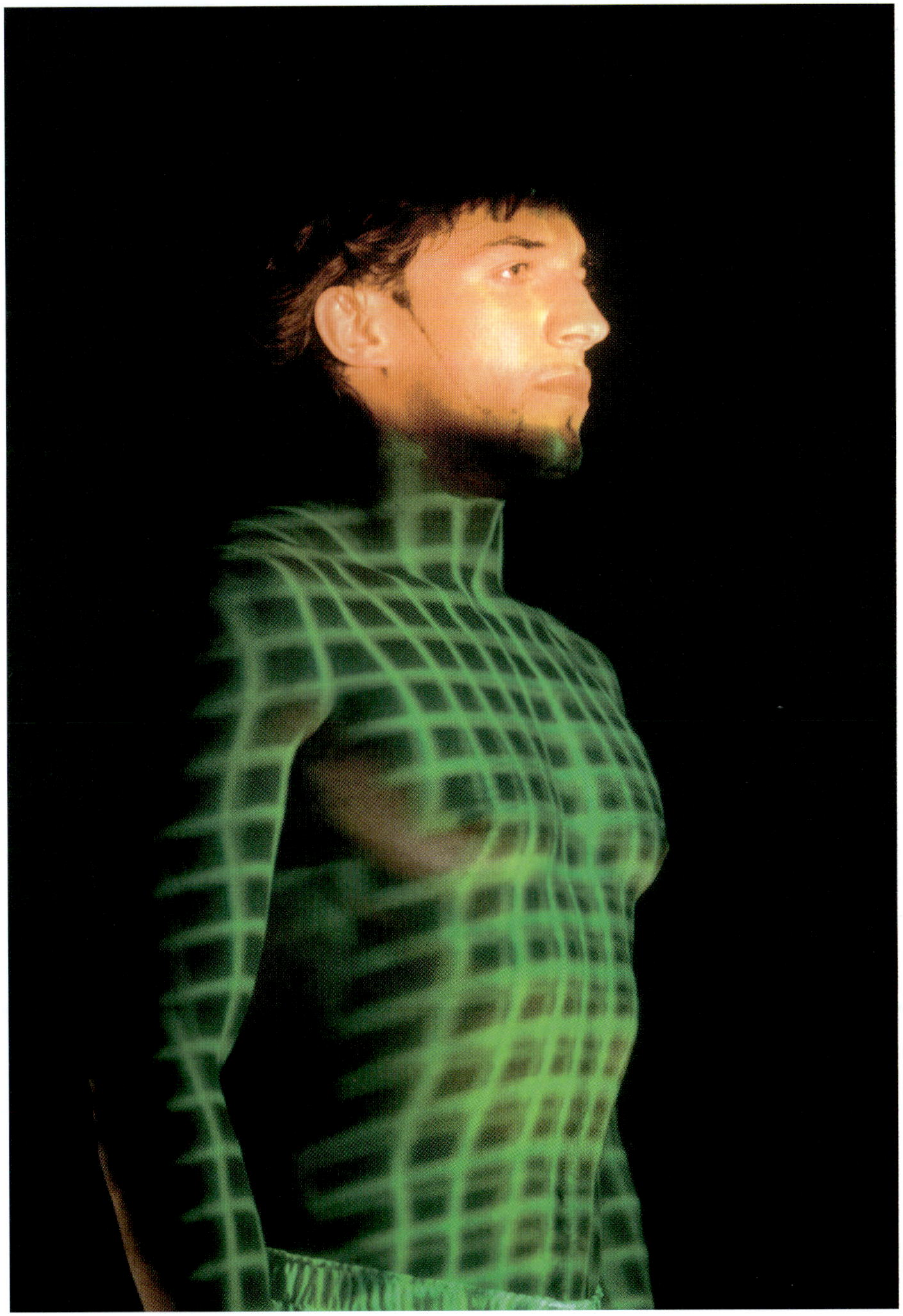

Left: Footballer as superbeing: Italian star Alessandro del Piero gets the hi-tech treatment in an advertisement for adidas filmed in March, 1997

Far left: 1966: fresh from lifting the World Cup, West Ham and England captain Bobby Moore strips off for the benefit of the Queen's couturier Sir Hardy Amies

Alpine Double-Glazing, by posing with Barbara Windsor. Years before appearing as Peggy Mitchell in *EastEnders*, Babs Windsor was the buxom darling of the *Carry On* films and many a football fan would have been delighted to see her face appear at their window.

Cut to 2002 and the latest England captain finds himself face to face with an even more buxom companion. Beckham: 6ft0in, 12 stone. Sumo wrestler: 6ft4in, 30 stone. But Beckham remains the heavyweight in the endorsement stakes. This head to head was all part of Pepsi's 'Share the Dream' campaign for the 2002 World Cup, which featured seven international superstars taking on a herd of sumos for the prize of a fridge full of the sugary soft drink.

Endorsements

ONE ICON GOOD, TWO ICONS BETTER. Anything that raises a smile is a good marketing device and, if you can get the England captain involved, so much the better. In 1970, Bobby Moore returned from the Mexico World Cup to do his bit for

Left: It's Bobby Moore again, this time after England failed to win the 1970 World Cup, teaming up with actress Babs Windsor to promote Alpine Double-Glazing

Below: As part of the build-up to the 2002 World Cup, Pepsi's 'Share the Dream' campaign brings David Beckham eyeball to eyeball with a sumo wrestler

Back home

HOME – THE ULTIMATE STATUS SYMBOL. When footballers were ordinary working men, just like the fans who went to see them play, they lived in terraced two-up, two-downs and got the bus to the ground just like everybody else.

But in the 1960s, after the abolition of the maximum wage, they suddenly found that they were rich and headed out into the stockbroker belt for a spot of house hunting. And the developers were ready for them, with a style of architecture designed to look 'olde-worlde' but with all the amenities to suit a race that stood at greater than five foot tall and had a taste for gadgets.

It was called Mock Tudor, and footballers lapped it up. In many cases, these houses were built in identical clusters, forming exclusive estates where footballers could live next door to one another and find their way around each other's homes as if they were their own. Only a handful rebelled. George Best had his own house built: a futuristic designer pad with lots of glass and concrete. But most remarkable of all was Eric Cantona, the king of Old Trafford in the 1990s, who was found to be living in a suburban semi at the height of his powers.

Right: January 11, 1972: George Best enjoys the privacy of his £30,000 luxury home in Bramhall, Cheshire, which he helped to design himself

Far right: Much-travelled goalkeeper Dave Beasant, who rose to fame in Wimbledon's FA Cup-winning side of 1988, outside his lovely home

KEEPERS COTTAGE

A game of two halves

BEHIND EVERY GREAT MAN IS A GRATEFUL WOMAN. Or something like that. As football has become more and more glamorous, so have the wives and girlfriends who watch – often with less than fervent enthusiasm – their other halves from the stands. While the female contingent among football crowds has risen considerably since the 1980s, it's remarkable how few footballers' partners are fans of the game.

What on earth can the attraction be? Managers always prefer to see their players married, believing it signals the end to all the distractions of bachelorhood that can detract from their game. If you know your full-back is at home mowing the lawn while his good lady keeps an eye on him from her lounger, you know he's not wasting his energy in the flesh pots of Soho, Manchester, Liverpool or Tyneside and will probably be fresh come Saturday afternoon. And in many cases the players oblige, getting married and having kids often in their early 20s, if not before. However, the attention that modern footballers attract from the opposite sex is hard for many to resist and the tabloids feed on a regular diet of kiss and tell stories featuring the stars of the game.

Left: Domestic bliss as modelled by Chelsea's Ron 'Chopper' Harris and his wife in 1970. For once, it was just the grass getting the chop

Right: David Ginola of Newcastle United, one of the Premiership's biggest heartthrobs, poses with future wife Coraline at a relaxed photo call in 1995

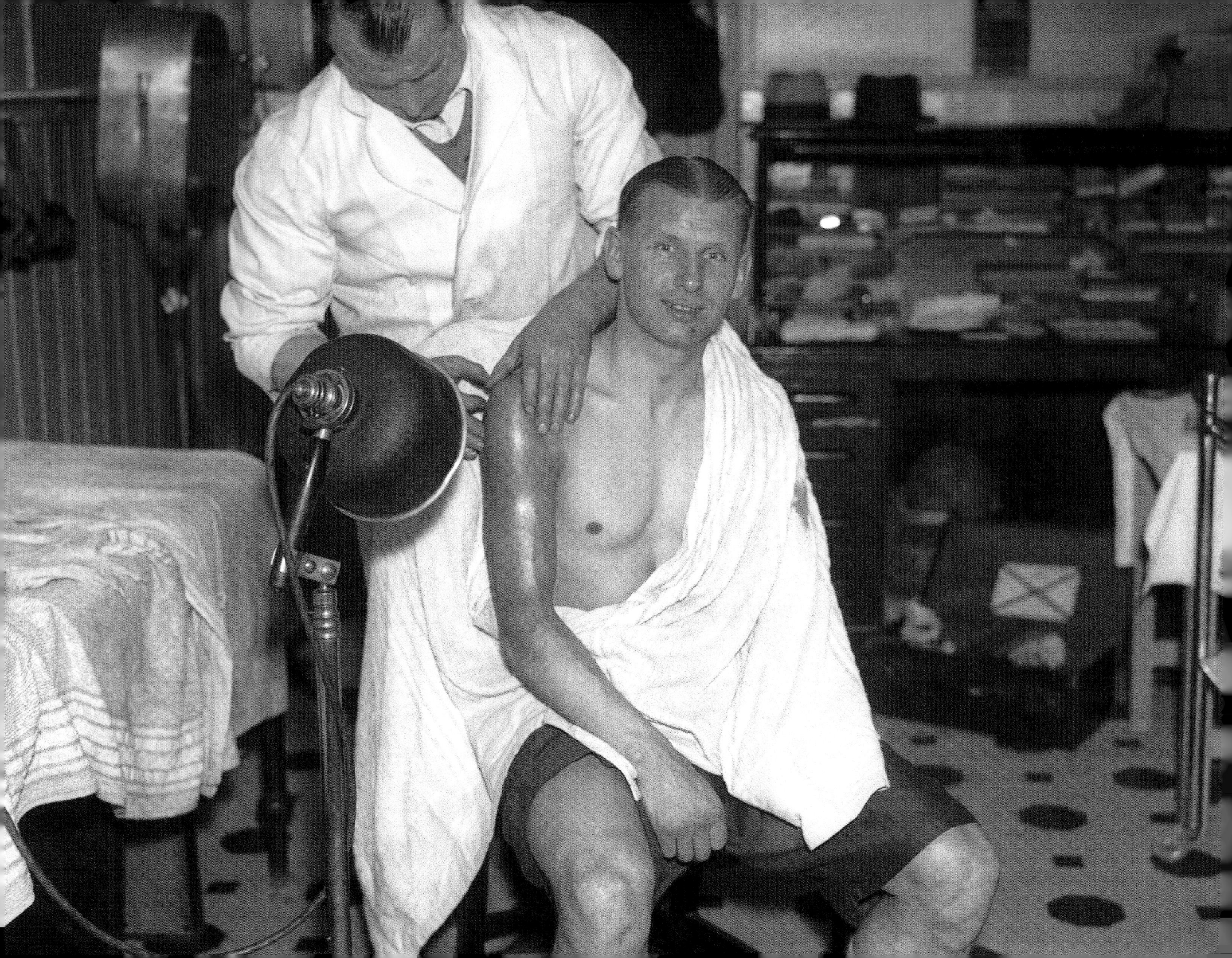

A little sunshine

FOOTBALL, BEING A WINTER GAME, is not blessed with a great deal of sunshine. After the bright and hopeful days of the beginning of the season, the game is played out beneath a blanket of cloud, rain and snow until May, when someone emerges out of the gloom to take the title and lift the Cup.

As a result, players get run down. Their batteries go flat. They need recharging. Physiotherapists have recognised the healing properties of sunlight for many years and made frequent use of sunlamps to speed up the recovery of injured players. Club tours to sunny climes – usually with a golf course on site – are a long-established feature of the team-building process and, if you study the board members at any top club, you're bound to find at least one with a stake in a villa in La Manga which he's happy to make available to the players.

It would have been difficult to let a player go on holiday during the season in the days before squad rotation systems, but now managers are inclined to send the odd player away for a top-up of sun if they're looking a bit jaded. A sun lamp would be cheaper, of course.

Left: Arsenal star Cliff Bastin undergoes treatment from a sun lamp to speed up the healing of his bruised shoulder, under the supervision of trainer Tom Whittaker in April, 1935

Right: Leeds striker Alan Smith and his girlfriend Laura Frain enter into the spirit of Walt Disney World while on holiday in Florida in June, 2002

Can she kick it?

DON'T LET ANYBODY TELL YOU FOOTBALL is a man's game. Women's football is the fastest growing sport in Britain. And in many countries, like the United States and Sweden, it challenges the men's game for popularity. In England, women's football has been going nearly as long as men's and, despite mixed football being banned by the FA in 1902, some men v women games took place during the First World War.

In 1921 women's teams were banned from using League grounds, a ruling that was only rescinded in the 1980s, by which time the Women's FA had been established and the WFA Cup well established. In 1992 a women's Premier League was set up, a year after the first Women's World Cup had seen the USA emerge as champions.

Professional women's football is now commonplace around the world, and Britain is catching up with the likes of Italy, the US and parts of Scandinavia. Whether the men's and women's games ever merge, with professional squads made up of both sexes, remains to be seen, but it seems unlikely. Indeed, with women's football flourishing in its own right, it seems unnecessary.

Left: Milene Dominguez, wife of Ronaldo and a keepie-uppie champion in her own right, shows skills to rival her husband's before a friendly match between the Italian club Monza and Region 4, a representative side from the west coast of America, on March 19, 2002

Far left: Players from Dagenham Docks and Hayes women's teams go up for a header during their Marine Cup match at Beacontree Heath on April 3, 1936

The boss

THE ROLE OF THE FOOTBALL MANAGER has been in a constant state of flux throughout the last one hundred years and the modern day 'gaffer' is a far cry from his Victorian counterpart. In fact, in the early days the position of manager had not been created and the task of team selection generally fell to the club secretary, who wouldn't have been exactly spoiled for choice.

In the early 20th century, the role of team manager was gradually established as being to take charge of team affairs. Even then, he tended to carry out his duties in a fairly hands-off capacity, seldom changing out of his suit. The concept of the 'tracksuit manager', who not only picked the players but coached and put them through their paces out on the training pitch, only came about in the 1950s.

As the manager's role brought him closer to the players, so the pressures of the job increased. Managers were seen as a disposable commodity and the threat of the sack made every result of the utmost importance. Today, managers differ in style – some laid back, some intense – but, successful or not, in all cases the pressure shows in the end.

Right: George Allison, manager of Arsenal from 1934 to 1947, looks relaxed and happy while he watches his side play a game on Christmas Eve, 1938

Far right: Liverpool manager Kenny Dalglish, wearing his kit under his trademark manager's coat, stands out from the crowd during the 1989 FA Cup Final against Everton

Candy

The impossible job

THE JOB OF ENGLAND MANAGER should be the most prestigious position in football. Being put in charge of the national team of the country that gave the game to the world – what higher accolade could there be? Yet during the managerial merry-go-round that saw the role change hands five times during the 1990s (seven, if you include caretakers), there was a spectacular absence of candidates pushing themselves forward for the job. Why? Well, it's the impossible job, isn't it? It probably doesn't help that the first man to manage England, as we understand that word today, went and won the World Cup.

Before Alf Ramsey, Walter Winterbottom was little more than a coach and administrator. He booked the hotels but had to defer to the FA on team selection. Ramsey had none of that, did his own thing and wrote his name in history. Ever since, England managers have crumbled under the weight of expectation, the best achievement being fourth in the 1990 World Cup under Bobby Robson. Eventually the FA decided to break with tradition and look abroad for a saviour. They came up with Sven-Goran Eriksson, a thoughtful Swede, but did anything change? No.

Left: Sir Alf Ramsey gazes into a crystal ball inscribed with the names of his World Cup-winning squad, a gift presented by Royal Brierley in September, 1966

Right: November 18, 2002: England manager Sven-Goran Eriksson in typically pensive pose, no doubt contemplating the conundrum of how to make England a world-beating force once again

It's a family affair

FOLLOWING IN THE FAMILY BUSINESS is a common feature in football. The question is, is it genes or is it nepotism? There are plenty of examples to suggest that certain families are clearly blessed with the football gene. The Charltons, for example, where brothers Bobby and Jack both played for England when they won the World Cup in 1966; their uncle, Jackie Milburn, had also won 13 caps for England and was the darling of Newcastle United. But there are also plenty of examples of former players becoming managers and, lo and behold, there's his son creeping into the first team but later failing to make the grade.

Sometimes, of course, the football gene strengthens in the younger generation. Michael Owen scores great goals in World Cup tournaments; his dad banged them in for Chester City. In a business where it's hard to get the breaks, it obviously helps to have your dad opening doors for you, but ultimately it's your own dedication and ability that determine whether or not you make the grade. What is rare is for both father and son to achieve greatness. The shadow of a superstar is very hard to emerge from.

Left: Paolo Maldini holds aloft the European Cup after his Milan side beat Barcelona 4–0 in the 1994 final, played in the Olympic Stadium in Athens

Far left: Milan captain Cesare Maldini holds up the European Cup after leading his side to victory, 2–1 over Benfica, in the 1963 final at Wembley

Charles Buchan's
1953-54
SOCCER
GIFT
BOOK

Who's the daddy?

THE 2000 FA CUP FINAL MADE HISTORY for a number of reasons. Not only was it the last Cup Final to take place at Wembley before shifting to Cardiff while the Mecca of football was rebuilt, it was also the first time a child had led the winning team up the Wembley steps to collect the trophy.

In a rather sweet display of parental pride, Chelsea captain Dennis Wise carried his young son with him as he went up to perform the famous ritual. For the traditionalists it was another blow to the game's oldest cup competition, which had already been demeaned by the non-participation of holders Manchester United. But most onlookers applauded the move, seeing it as a confirmation of the sensitive, caring, family-oriented nature that the game had supposedly taken on since the formation of the Premiership and the introduction of all-seater stadiums.

In years gone by, children only appeared on the field of play when invading the pitch. Famous players might allow a photographer to shoot them with their family every once in a while, but when it came to match day it was time to leave childish things behind.

Left: Bedtime in the Matthews household in 1953 and wing wizard Stanley Matthews reads *Charles Buchan's Soccer Gift Book* to his son Stanley Jnr

Right: Chelsea captain Dennis Wise breaks with tradition after winning the 2000 FA Cup Final and carries his son, Henry, up with him to collect the famous trophy

The festive season

CHRISTMAS IS A VERY SIGNIFICANT STAGE in the football calendar, falling as it does around the mid-way point in the season, with a busy fixture schedule that is said to dictate success or failure for the remainder of the season. While it may not be a clear indicator of who will win the League, teams who are bottom at Christmas seldom survive the drop come May. For the players it is one of the hardest times of year, not just because of all the games but because, while everyone else is enjoying time with their family, Christmas Day has to be spent away at a hotel, preparing for the Boxing Day fixture.

In order to make up for the heartache of the Christmas period, clubs traditionally organise a party and the players usually turn up in fancy dress. In recent years many of these club parties have degenerated into drunken chaos and players have had to spend many hours in the manager's office afterwards, explaining why their picture has appeared on the back pages of the tabloids showing them in a compromising position with at least one member of the opposite sex. Still, it's usually forgotten about by New Year.

Right: Two days before Christmas in 1936, Liverpool players Bradshaw and Hobson put up the decorations in the hotel in Rhyl where they are staying with the team

Far right: Chris Waddle (left) performs his famous Stan Laurel impression and Paul Gascoigne adopts the more portly role as the Geordie heroes get into the Christmas spirit at Tottenham, Christmas, 1989

Two:

Theatres of dreams

Right: The River Plate stadium, Buenos Aires, in 1978 as it prepared for the World Cup final between Argentina and Holland, which ended 3–1 to the hosts

1955

The ground

THE MOST OBVIOUS MEASURE of the growth of football since the first organised games in the 19th century is the bricks and mortar. Early football grounds could hardly be called stadiums, comprising as they did a pitch and little else. Changing rooms were often the toilets of the local pub. Spectators were an afterthought.

But, having realised that there were plenty of interested followers to fill them, soon ambitious club-owners started building stands. In the early part of the 20th century, the bigger clubs were building proper stadiums, with a consistent basic design that involved covered stands along the sides of the pitch and open terraces at each end. If you wanted comfort, you sat in the stands; if you wanted atmosphere and were prepared to suffer the rain, you stood on the terraces.

During the boom years after World War II, stadiums quickly grew to accommodate the swelling crowds. Some, like Old Trafford, became modern-looking arenas, with a roof on all four sides intensifying the noise and atmosphere of the terraces. But the Hillsborough disaster in 1989 spelt the end of terracing at major grounds and ushered in the all-seater age. Now, in the era of multi-tiered mega-stadiums, the only thing that suffers is the grass because the sun and wind barely reach it.

Above: The majestic curves of the Big Eye stadium in Oita, Japan, form the backdrop as Senegal celebrate Henri Camara's goal against Sweden in the World Cup on June 16, 2002

Left: No sweeping roofs here, just single-tier stands, terraces and a smoking factory chimney set the scene at Bradford Park Avenue for the visit of Wrexham on April 2, 1955

Let there be light

APPROACHING AN UNFAMILIAR STADIUM for the first time, there used to be three ways of knowing which direction to head in: 1, follow the crowds; 2, ask a policeman; 3, look for the floodlight pylons. It didn't have to be night time, even unlit, the old-style floodlights towered so high above the ground that they were generally the first sign that you were getting close. They were also responsible for a sight that used to be so familiar but now is a thing of the past: the four-man shadow. Because they were generally positioned in each corner of the stadium, the floodlights cast four shadows of each player as they shone down. It was part of the heightened atmosphere of night games, which were more often than not cup games.

The first floodlit football match was played way back in 1878 at Bramall Lane, Sheffield, but it wasn't until November 1955 that they were first used in the FA Cup, with the first floodlit League match taking place between Portsmouth and Newcastle on February 22, 1956. Today, floodlights are mounted at lower level, usually on the stand roof, and bathe the entire playing area in an even light.

Right: May 6, 1967: West Ham's temporary goalkeeper, Mackleworth, grabs the ball from under Denis Law's nose and within sight of Upton Park's towering floodlight pylons, typical of the lights that served as landmarks at almost every ground

Far right: Powerful floodlights mounted along the roof of the San Siro stadium light the whole place up as Dennis Wise takes a corner for Chelsea against AC Milan in October 1999

WISE
11
PlayStat

·R
RVED·

1974

Making a meal of it

NOW THAT FOOTBALL CLUBS REGARD all their supporters as a potential revenue source, the refreshment facilities available have been upgraded to an enormous degree. Once upon a time you'd do well to get a cup of Bovril and a bag of roasted chestnuts; today you can get a three-course meal, complete with the club's own-label wine. That is, of course, if you can afford it.

While the average fan has become more affluent, or at least more prone to spending money on the club, the clubs themselves have gone out of their way to attract the growing band of wealthy supporters who now see football as an excellent alternative to the golf course when it comes to wooing clients. Lavish hospitality packages that suit the corporate entertainer down to the ground are offered at all levels of the professional game.

Many a deal is done over a prawn sandwich and a glass of United Red in the Old Trafford hospitality suite, hopefully leaving time to look out of the window and catch the last five minutes of the match. Even for the fans who can't afford the hospitality suites, the choice – if not always the quality – of food and drink has improved, with major fast-food chains opening up franchises in several stadiums.

Left: Two Newcastle United fans, one wearing possibly the world's tallest hat, brew up on a camping stove outside Wembley, having failed to get tickets for the 1974 FA Cup Final against Liverpool

Right: April 19, 2003: corporate hospitality at Goodison before the Liverpool derby which the hosts lost 2–1

1914

Getting a view

AS FOOTBALL MOVED UPMARKET in the wake of the Taylor Report, which put conditions for football spectators under the microscope following the Hillsborough disaster, there was a general realisation amongst the people running the clubs that changes were required.

The chain reaction began with the ruling that stadiums must be all-seater. This meant ground capacities, and therefore attendances, would fall, which in turn meant that fans would have to be charged more to gain admission. If they wanted to charge more without losing their core support, the clubs would have to improve the offering for the paying customer and, in most cases, that meant giving them a decent view of the game.

When football was cheap, fans were happy to crane their necks, or find their own vantage points – the toilet window, a floodlight pylon etc – but once they'd been forced to sit in one place it became apparent just how bad the view was in many grounds.

The introduction of jumbo screens began as a form of half-time entertainment: the image quality was poor and they were not permitted to show the action during play. But now the screens are of much better quality and can ensure that you always get a decent view of what's going on. And they have replays too, if you do happen to miss any of the action.

Left: Fans perch on poles at the Crystal Palace in an effort to catch a glimpse of the 1914 FA Cup Final between Burnley and Liverpool. Burnley won 1–0

Right: Nowhere to hide for Manchester United goal-keeper Fabien Barthez, as his image fills the giant screen at Highbury during defeat by Arsenal in November, 2001

1897

Cup Final day

THE OLDEST CUP COMPETITION IN FOOTBALL saw its first final in 1872, played between Wanderers and Royal Engineers at Kennington Oval, now the home of Surrey County Cricket Club. Wanderers won 1–0 and went on to lift the famous cup a further four times that decade. The FA Cup Final was played at a variety of grounds in its early years, but the Oval was the most used venue until it was switched to Crystal Palace in 1895. This wasn't on the site of Selhurst Park, the home of Crystal Palace FC, but up the hill at the Crystal Palace itself, which is today the home of the athletics stadium. As you can see from this picture, it wasn't an ideal venue for the thousands who flocked to south London for such a big game, yet it remained the venue for the final until 1914.

When the competition resumed after the hostilities of World War I, the final was held for three years at Stamford Bridge, before moving to the newly built Wembley stadium for the legendary White Horse Final of 1923. On that occasion, overcrowding almost prevented the match taking place at all, but Wembley still became the spiritual home of the FA Cup Final and remains so, despite temporary removal to the Millennium Stadium, Cardiff, while the old Mecca of football is rebuilt.

Above: May 20, 2000: pitchside for the last FA Cup Final to be played at Wembley before the developers move in. Chelsea beat Aston Villa 1–0

Left: The pitch seems miles away for fans trying to watch the 1897 FA Cup Final between Aston Villa and Everton at the Crystal Palace. Villa won the match 3–2

The tunnel

ONE OF THE HIGH POINTS of going to any game is the moment when the players emerge from the tunnel. Or, to be more precise, the moments just before the players emerge. The anticipation builds, every fan preparing to give full vent to his passion in support of his team, every eye straining for that first glimpse of colour.

The extent to which the anticipation grows depends largely on the design of the tunnel. In most British stadiums, the tunnels slope gently up to pitch level and it is possible to see a little way in, to spot the occasional flash of a sock or a ball as the players line up outside the dressing-rooms. In other countries, the tunnels open up from the ground and the teams suddenly burst out into the light, the only forewarning being the emergence of the ball boys.

Emerging from and returning to the tunnel, the players come closest to the fans and it has become the scene of much back-slapping and congratulation... but also of considerable abuse. Consequently, many tunnels are now covered over to a point where the fans no longer get a tantalising glimpse of the players and some of the thrill has gone.

Right: Newcastle full-back Frank Hodspeth leaves the Wembley pitch clutching the FA Cup after his side's 2–0 victory over Aston Villa in 1924

Far right: Players and officials share a joke in the tunnel before Ecuador's match against Mexico in the 1997 Copa America at Cochabamba, Bolivia

6
adidas
PENALTY

1919

Architectural art

WHEN THE WORLD CUP CAME TO ASIA for the first time ever in 2002, the host nations Japan and South Korea seized the opportunity to demonstrate their prowess in design technology and built 19 brand new, state-of-the-art stadiums between them. A far cry from the simple terraces and picket fences of the pre-war years, each of these stadiums was designed to catch the eye and add to the awe-inspiring spectacle of the tournament. All the latest technological developments were on display: retractable roofs, retractable pitches, earthquake resistance... but the designs themselves broke new ground. This was football stadium as art. One was supposed to make spectators feel like they were entering a whirlpool, another was built to represent a ship in full sail, another a bird in flight. Despite the fact that there was no projected use for many of these stadiums after the World Cup, Japan and South Korea spent a total of £4 billion in building them.

Their effect in lending spectacular edge to the tournament was unquestionable, but there's something about those simple grounds of the past, where the crowd created its own atmosphere, that all the money in the world can't seem to capture today.

Above: The massed red shirts of South Korean fans add colour to the graceful lines of the Gwangju stadium for their side's World Cup quarter-final against Spain in June 2002

Left: The massed crowds of fans, all dressed alike, are held back by a white picket fence as they watch Millwall play Reading in September, 1919

1955

The San Siro

ITALY IS ANOTHER COUNTRY that took its hosting of the World Cup as an opportunity to rebuild many of its stadiums. One of the most famous examples is the Giuseppe Meazza stadium in Milan, also known as the San Siro. First built in 1926, this giant bowl is shared by the city's two great clubs, Internazionale and AC Milan. At one stage it had a capacity of 150,000, although the Milanese council restricted it to 100,000 for safety reasons. The rebuilding in 1989, for the World Cup the following year, saw the addition of an imposing glass-fibre roof and 11 spiralling stair towers, which give it the look of a massive space craft that has come to land on the outskirts of the city.

Capacity was cut to 85,000, all seated on concrete steps. Inside, the San Siro is one of the most imposing stadiums in the world. Built specifically for football, the stands tower up close to the pitch and when the fans of the *Rossoneri* (AC Milan) or the *Nerazzuri* (Inter) are in full cry, it is a cauldron of noise, colour and fire from the flares.

Above: The awesome San Siro stadium, home to both Milan clubs and redeveloped for the 1990 World Cup, stands like a huge spaceship on the outskirts of the city

Left: Milan's Giuseppe Meazza stadium, aka the San Siro, in 1955, roofless but huge, with a capacity of well over 100,000 at its peak

1923

The Twin Towers

FOOTBALL HAS UNDERGONE innumerable subtle changes since it first became an organised sport over a hundred years ago, but few of those changes have provoked as much passionate debate as the demolition of Wembley's Twin Towers. The towers, which were actually little more than a couple of domes rising up on either side of the main entrance to the stadium, constituted arguably the most recognisable landmark in football. To fans the world over they symbolised something sacred: Wembley, the Mecca of football.

To continue the analogy, the demolition of the Twin Towers – a consequence of the rebuilding programme set in motion at the turn of the millennium – was, in the eyes of the traditionalists, akin to tearing down the Wailing Wall or the Taj Mahal.

Surely some way could be found to incorporate these world-famous structures within the design of the new stadium. Alas, no such solution had been found when the cranes moved in, in 2003, and began to pick the Twin Towers apart, like vultures feeding off the carcass of an elephant. In their place, the new Wembley would be marked out by a huge arch, visible for miles around.

Right: A landmark is born. The Twin Towers near completion on the newly built Empire Stadium, Wembley, in time for the 1923 FA Cup Final

Far right: February 12, 2003: after 80 years standing as a symbol of the home of football, the Twin Towers of Wembley are picked apart by the demolition men

McGEE
McGEE
M43

1967

On the bench

THE BENCH USED TO BE A LONELY PLACE for a manager. It probably still is, given that they spend most games in a world of their own, but in physical terms they have more company during the 90 minutes of play than anyone would have imagined 50 years ago.

Back then substitutes were only permitted in friendlies and it was generally you and your assistant, who doubled as bucket-and-sponge man. If a player went down injured and the magic sponge didn't do the trick, you were down to 10 men: no questions, no decisions, no shuffling of the pack.

Substitutes were introduced at the beginning of the 1965–66 season, one only, to be used to replace an injured player. The number gradually crept up and the rules changed to allow tactical substitutions. Then substitute goalkeepers were allowed, largely in response to tighter laws that were causing more goalkeepers to be sent off for the 'professional foul'. Today you're allowed five subs on the bench, of which you can use three. Where once a club's reserve team was very much secondary to the first team, now the distinction is barely detectable, with clubs run on a squad basis – and much bigger benches required.

Above: Seven (count them) players and nearly as many coaching and medical staff populate the Arsenal bench during their Champions League match against Barcelona in the Nou Camp, September, 1999

Left: In a tiny dugout, accompanied only by his trainer, Tommy Docherty watches his Rotherham side play at Millwall on November 25, 1967

1938

Bath time

IT'S SOMETIMES EASY TO FORGET, with so many individual players hyped up to be superstars, that football is a game in which team spirit is a vital ingredient for success. But there's something about seeing these 'gods' in the bath or shower that brings them back down to earth. The team bath often played a key role in the team-building process: a place to celebrate or commiserate together; to relax, laugh, sing, unwind as a team. It was unselfconscious, communal, basic. Today, players would balk at being photographed bathing together, even if the communal bath hadn't been replaced in most instances by showers or individual tubs. And they would certainly be shy about being photographed smoking.

That is not to say that modern players don't smoke – Robert Prosinecki, one of the stars of the Croatia team of the 1990s, was reputedly on 50 a day – but the increased awareness of the harmful effects of smoking, coupled with the emphasis on presenting a wholesome image, particularly for young fans, means they are seldom caught doing it. What's more, it's much harder to smoke in the shower.

Left: Ipswich players think nothing of lighting up a cigarette as they relax in the team bath following an FA Cup replay against Aston Villa in 1938

Right: A young Diego Maradona appears to have been caught a little by surprise as he washes his hair after a game in November, 1980

Three:
Come all ye faithful

Right: All-male Sheffield Wednesday fans watch the game from the terraces during the early stages of WWII – flat caps were about to be exchanged for tin helmets

1949

Fanatics

FOOTBALL FANS HAVE ALWAYS been prone to bouts of eccentricity. Loyalty to the team seems to awaken the tribal instinct in all of us, and that manifests itself in extrovert displays of colour, noise and movement.

The basic instinct hasn't changed over the years, but the method has. For the rattle-waving fan of the 1940s, the idea of bodypaint would have been hilarious. Something for the avant-garde art movements, perhaps. But today, bodypainting of some description – usually limited to the face – is quite normal among fans, particularly when the major international tournaments come around and the pageantry reaches its peak.

The football rattle used to be as common at matches as hot dogs and Bovril, but these weighty lumps of wood, designed for no other purpose than to make a hell of racket, started being used as offensive weapons in the hooligan-blighted era of the 1970s and 1980s and were consequently banned.

In latter years, harmless versions made out of bouncy foam were invented, but the day of the rattle had died, and the new way to express your love for your team was to paint yourself in their colours.

Left: Leicester City fan George Hughes, in London for a cup tie against Brentford in February, 1949, demonstrates the full noise capacity of his rattles

Right: A Ghana fan, painted with the colours of his national flag, at the African Nations Cup tournament held in Nigeria in 2000

1936

Sign here please

PROFESSIONAL FOOTBALLERS ARE TAUGHT to respect autograph-hunters. In a game that is often criticised for the gulf in status between the supporters and their idols, it is an old ritual that is seen as part of the process of giving something back to the fans. But as players have been built up into bigger and bigger stars, especially in the eyes of children, it is a demand that has risen beyond control. Whereas once you would see a famous player trailed by a handful of straggling kids proffering paper and pen as he made his way to his car, now it is a sea of young faces that engulfs any player who ventures into the public domain.

The collectability of autographs has also created a market, and many of the 'faithful' flocking round the stars will actually be stockpiling signatures for sale. This demand can put a real strain on the modern footballer, especially if his name's Thomas Hitzelsberger. Practising your autograph is now part of the young footballer's development. You need something that's stylish yet quick to write and preferably illegible. And it needs to be different to the way you sign your cheques.

Right: Autograph-hunters at The Valley, home of Charlton Athletic, try to cajole the players into signing as they pause during a pre-season training run in July, 1936

Far right: August 1, 2000, and new kit launch pulls in the crowds. Manchester United and Republic of Ireland full-back Denis Irwin finds hmself surrounded by autograph-hunters on the concourse at Old Trafford

IRWIN
3

1935

Football train

TRAINS HAVE ALWAYS BEEN A POPULAR form of transport for football fans but the levels of comfort and speed have altered somewhat. In Britain they seem to have got slower and more uncomfortable. When football was still regarded as working-class entertainment and few fans travelled to the match by car, the railways laid on football specials to ferry them to away games. These trains would often be where the pre-match atmosphere got going, as fans enjoyed a drink and a sing-song without having to worry about who was driving.

In the 1970s, though, the football specials often arrived at their destination with the seats ripped out and lights smashed. The hooligans had taken over. Football specials became extinct for all but the major games and fans began to take to the road.

But Japan has a train service to be proud of and, when the World Cup took place there in 2002, fans were treated to the high-tech pleasures of the famous Bullet Train. This fan, wearing an England shirt with the name of the captain emblazoned across the back, is actually Japanese – one of an army of Far Eastern fans who adopted the stars of English football as their heroes during the tournament.

Left: Two confident-looking Manchester City fans aboard a special train from Euston to White Hart Lane *en route* to a 1935 cup tie against Tottenham Hotspur

Right: June, 2002 and a dejected-looking Japanese fan in an England shirt waits to board the Bullet Train after England's World Cup defeat to Brazil in Shizuoka

BECKHAM
7
10

Colours

THESE PICTURES CAPTURE the extreme difference between the look of the old-fashioned football crowd and the look of the crowd today. The old picture may be in black and white, but if it had been taken in colour the only difference would be the sky. People really did dress in monochrome, topped off with a flat cap for throwing in the air. When they talk about 'the people's game', these were 'the people'. Note the young boy being passed down to the front.

Today, fans still tend to dress alike, but there is a greater sense of self-expression and participation in the spectacle. This is largely due to the influence of Latin America and Africa on the footballing world. Unlike the British workers who trooped out of the factories on Saturday lunchtime and marched off to the match just to watch, smoke Woodbines and swear a bit, on other continents the growth of football offered an opportunity to express their natural *joie de vivre*.

The concept of wearing your colours became big in Britain in the 1960s, in the form of scarves and bobble hats, but the growth of hooliganism frightened a lot of fans into hiding their loyalties. By the late 1980s, fans felt safer again and the fashion for replica shirts took off.

Above: Modern tournaments bring a dazzling array of colour with them, as demonstrated by these Togo fans in Nigeria for the 2000 African Nations Cup

Left: On the packed terraces at West Ham in 1930, the uniform is flat caps and working clothes. Notice the boy being passed over the heads of the crowd – a tradition long gone

Vantage point

FANS HAVE ALWAYS GONE to extraordinary lengths to get a glimpse of the match, sometimes with disastrous results. In 1987 a Wolves supporter fell through the roof at Scarborough while watching the opening game of the season with several of his fellow supporters from the highest vantage point in the ground. In those days, the police fought a constant battle to stop people climbing up the roof supports and floodlight pylons, but once anybody had started to gain height, as these fans had at Cardiff City, it became very hard to get them down.

Modern stadiums are designed without any obvious climbing apparatus, but fans that can't get in, like these Zambia supporters, still show tremendous courage, ingenuity and dedication to the cause.

And they're only watching their team in training. Imagine what it would be like if there were a match on! Trees, cranes, neighbouring office blocks and flats, they've all been used to gain a free view of the match, but with more and more modern, enclosed stadiums being built, the days of precarious vantage points could soon be at an end.

Above: Zambian fans pile up rickety stacks of building blocks to look over the stadium wall as their national team trains in 1994

Left: March 5, 1921, and a huge crowd watch Cardiff City play Chelsea, a number of them climbing on to the unfinished roof of the stand for a precarious vantage point

Celebrity fans

FOOTBALL HAS ALWAYS ATTRACTED an element of famous support but in the recent, glamorous age of the Premiership, it has become something of a badge of honour for 'celebs' of all descriptions. This is regarded with some irony by the 'ordinary' fans who found themselves somewhat ostracised during the 1970s and 80s, when football was associated with hooliganism and yobbishness. Now, having remained silent throughout those years, whole swathes of TV personalities are eagerly claiming they were there all along.

Whereas today you can hardly move around Highbury or Stamford Bridge without feeling like you've stumbled into the Groucho Club, when you look back through history it's easy to spot the famous fans that wore their colours through thick and thin.

And most of them were comedians. Tommy Trinder served his time as chairman of Fulham, Peter Cook based some of his finest moments around his experiences at Tottenham ("I was down Spurs the other day when this bloke come up to me and said, 'Hello.'") and Eric Morecambe, bizarrely but resolutely, supported Luton. But probably most vocal of them all was, and still is, Rod Stewart. All together now... "You're Celtic, United but baby I've decided you're the best team I've ever seen."

Right: Pop star Rod Stewart, one of Scotland's most famous fans, dons the tartan in support of his team, who beat England 2–0 in May 1974

Far right: September 1, 2001: Rod the Mod takes his place among the Scotland fans again. This time, it's for a World Cup qualifier against Croatia, which ended 0–0

1977

Tartan army

BEATING ENGLAND HAS ALWAYS been the top priority for Scotland, both on the field and off it. The Auld Enemy came face to face in the first-ever international match in 1872 – a 0–0 draw played out in Glasgow – and they've met over a hundred times since, with honours more or less even.

The Home Internationals (a four-way tournament also involving Wales and Northern Ireland) provided England v Scotland as an annual fixture and the Scots always relished playing away. It was a chance to march on London, to dance in the fountains of Trafalgar Square and to take over Wembley to the extent that hardly an English voice could be heard or an English flag spotted in the 100,000 crowd.

They were dubbed the Tartan Army. But in 1977 their exuberance spilled over, when a 2–1 win at Wembley prompted them to invade the pitch, dig up the turf and break down the goals. It spelt the end of the Home Internationals and forced the Tartan Army to go through an image change. As England fans built a world-wide reputation as hooligans, the Scots went the other way, priding themselves on their good behaviour, if only to be different from the Sassenachs. Today the Tartan Army are welcome anywhere – as, alas, are their team, who have become a rather soft touch.

Left: The infamous pitch invasion by the Tartan Army at Wembley on June 4, 1977, after Scotland beat England 2–1 in the Home Internationals

Right: November 13, 1999, and disappointed Scotland fans leave Hampden Park after losing 2–0 to England in a Euro 2000 play-off match

Young fans

EVERY DAD HOPES THAT HIS SON will grow up supporting the same team he does. In fact, so abhorrent is the thought of one's own offspring supporting the wrong team, that many parents put their children's football education ahead of education itself. But at what price?

'Taking the lad to the match' is no longer the natural rite of passage that it once was, where you paid a few pence to get him through the junior turnstiles, stood him on a tea crate so he could see, or passed him over the heads of the crowd to the front. As the thousands drifted away after the final whistle, all the dads would relocate their pride and joy from amongst the litter and wander homeward, chatting merrily about the great players they had just seen.

Today, if you want to take your kids to the match you have to save up as if you're saving for a holiday. On top of the match ticket, which won't be much cheaper than your own, if at all, they'll want the replica shirt, a programme, the hat, the duvet cover and a drink and a bite to eat at half-time. All told, you'll be lucky to come away with change from £100.

Above: 1947: it was tough being a young boy on the packed terraces of the post-war era. Here two lads get passed down to the front to watch Chelsea v Arsenal

Right: 1996: a young Chelsea fan, kitted out in replica shirt and club hat, waits patiently at an empty Stamford Bridge for the game against Newcastle United

1970

Banter

THERE ARE PARTS OF THE GROUND where players can't avoid some kind of contact with the crowd, even if it is only verbal. They will tell you that they blot out the sound of the crowd when they're playing, but sometimes that's impossible. Goalkeepers are particularly vulnerable and need to have a good sense of humour when defending the goal in front of the opposition supporters. There will always be the odd fan – usually with a voice like a foghorn – who prides himself on his ability to distract certain players with a well-chosen remark.

Even the introduction of strict laws controlling offensive language won't stop the wit who doesn't rely on swearing to get inside the head of his chosen victim. In the thick of the action it's easy to ignore such calls from the crowd, but when play breaks down, that's when the message comes across. Try taking a corner when a voice six feet away from you is delivering a stream of abuse into your ear. Following his dismissal in the 1998 World Cup, David Beckham had to tolerate this situation everywhere he went. The fact that he stood the test, and indeed continued to shine, won him the respect of fans from all clubs.

Right: The sixth round of the FA Cup on February 21, 1970, and Watford's Barry Endean is cheered by young fans on the way to a 1–0 victory over Liverpool

Far right: A Chelsea fan gives David Beckham the benefit of his wisdom as he prepares to take a corner in Manchester United's 5–3 victory in the FA Cup third round in 1998 – you can almost hear what he's saying

SHARP
CHELSEA
CAL

On the box

ONCE UPON A TIME, if you wanted to see the match, you had no alternative but to go to the game. Then came television. The first match to be beamed into people's living rooms was in 1937. Even so, it took half a century for television to become the influential force in football that it is today. Until the 1980s, the only games you could expect to see live on television were cup finals and internationals. Live football was a rarity, a treat, a reason for whole communities to gather round a single black-and-white TV set and try to make sense of the tiny figures running around on the fuzzy screen.

Today, you can catch the game while powdering your nose in the hotel toilet. Television practically controls football. In Britain alone you can see three live games on any given weekend during the season, and major tournaments such as the European Champions League and the World Cup are scheduled to suit the television audience. With the broadcast rights for the 2002 and 2006 World Cups selling for £1.17 billion, it's no wonder the TV companies insist on a certain degree of control. But the influence of television appears to have peaked. By 2003, the tide of money flooding into the game from television was rapidly receding.

Left: As Manchester United play Blackpool in the 1948 FA Cup Final, Rediffusion invite subscribers to their London office to watch it live on television

Right: October 13, 1993: there's no need to miss a single kick these days. A visitor to the Jurys hotel in Dublin watches the Republic of Ireland play Spain with only the lavatory attendant for company

CLERYS

1950

Street football

THE CLASSIC BRITISH FOOTBALLER learned his skills in the streets, between rows of terraced houses with jumpers for goalposts. Bobby Charlton developed his thunderous shot by kicking the ball against a wall over and over again, until power and accuracy became second nature.

Today, you can't play football in Britain's streets without running the risk of getting hit by a car. For a long time, kids struggled to find somewhere else to practise and the basic development of the British player suffered. Not enough kids were playing; the base of the pyramid became too small, the peak too low.

Today, professional clubs invest heavily in soccer academies, where kids can go to get top-level coaching from an early age. The benefits are beginning to show. Meanwhile, in parts of the world where there is still a culture for playing the basic 'street' game, football is booming. The Copacabana beach in Rio is the most famous breeding ground for world-class footballers, but the towns and villages of Africa are rapidly churning out their own stars of the future. Such is the beauty of football, that the World Cup final can be re-enacted move for move on the dusty roads of Soweto.

Above: The beauty of football lies in its simplicity; it can be played anywhere with a minimum of equipment. These Zambian kids are lost in a game in their village street in 1993

Left: A sight seldom seen in Britain these days, especially London: a bunch of kids play between the houses in a 1950s East End street, with jumpers for goalposts

The power of the brand

SINCE THE SECOND WORLD WAR and the boom in attendances at football that followed, fans have always sought ways to show their allegiance to the team. It began as simply wearing the colours – a hat, scarf or rosette – and developed to badges and, occasionally, shirts. After a while sports shops started selling enamel and sew-on badges that said things like 'United – Ace of Clubs' with a playing card design, and fans would pin or sew these on to their scarves or hats. But nobody was making much money out of it. Then, just as the bad old 1980s were drawing to an end, football came into fashion.

Fans wouldn't just wear their club's shirt to the match; they'd wear it out to clubs and raves. And as the younger market followed suit, the clubs finally cottoned on to the fact that they had a huge money-spinner in the palm of their hands. The Manchester United merchandise business grew almost overnight from a small shop on the corner of the concourse to a vast enterprise comprising a megastore, a superstore and countless branded outlets throughout Britain and the world, bankrolling the purchase of new players who in turn boosted the profits in the shops. The power of the brand had come into its own.

Above: August 17, 2002: mannequins stand in line at the Manchester United Megastore outside Old Trafford, each modelling the latest replica kit for an army of hungry consumers

Left: Tottenham Hotspur souvenirs, including pin badges, miniature cups and pennants, on sale during a tour of the United States in July, 1952

Four:

They also serve...

Right: A small army of sweepers attempts to clear the pitch at White Hart Lane during the cold winter of 1948 – some years before the advent of undersoil heating

The draw

AS FOOTBALL HAS EVOLVED and grown to be known as 'the World game', rituals have developed, which form part of the great tradition of the sport. The FA Cup draw is one of the oldest and most compelling of all these formal ceremonies, governing, as it does, the oldest cup competition in the world. Until the television-dominated era of the late 20th century, it was a somewhat sombre ritual, carried out by two Football Association dignitaries with a bag of wooden balls. The sound of those balls knocking together would evoke a Pavlovian feeling of excitement in all fans whose team was still in the draw. "Hereford United... will play Newcastle..."

Sensing that they had the makings of a great TV moment, the FA allowed this great ritual to be jazzed up, replacing the bag of wooden balls with what looked like a food blender full of ping-pong balls. And they drafted in a couple of ex-pros to pull them out. Unsurprisingly, it added nothing to the atmosphere of the event. The World Cup draw becomes a more and more elaborate affair with each passing tournament, as FIFA strive to achieve a spectacle befitting such a huge event. In the end, though, all that really matters is the names that come out. 1, Germany; 2, England. Enough said.

Left: FA Challenge Cup Committee chairman David Wiseman (left) and FA vice-president RH Brough solemnly draw Millwall v Spurs in the FA Cup, January, 1967

Right: Celebrity sumo wrestler Konishiki looms large as the theatrical World Cup qualifying draw on December 7, 1999, puts England in the same group as Germany

UEFA
GROUP
9
1 GERMANY
2 ENGLAND
3 GREECE
4 FINLAND
5 ALBANIA
2002 FIFA WORLD CUP
KOREA JAPAN
POT C
POT A
FIFA
POT B
POT D

1922

Preparing the surface

THE GROUNDSMAN HAS ALWAYS PLAYED a key role in football. Home advantage is about more than just having the crowd behind you, it's being familiar with the playing area: the surface, the dimensions, the proximity of the crowd. Managers will use any advantage they can gain over their opponents, and one of the first things they look at is how the pitch suits their style of play. If they like to use the wings, he can reduce the width of the pitch; if they like to play quick, passing football, he can order the pitch to be left a bit bumpy and have it heavily watered before the game.

It may sound unsporting, but it's part of the game and it means the groundsman can be a manager's key player. Preparing playing surfaces has become a real science, especially since stadium designers started building bowls with no openings between the stands. Normal grass suffers from the lack of wind and sun, so special hybrid grasses have been developed that are more robust. For more and more stadiums today, however, the only way to maintain a good playing surface is to have the turf re-laid on a regular basis, sometimes two or three times a season.

Left: A groundsman relies on horsepower to level the goalmouth with the heavy roller, ready for the start of the season in August 1922

Right: Beneath the retractable roof of the Millennium Stadium, Cardiff, the groundsman gives the grass a quick trim in preparation for the 2002 FA Cup Final

Programme seller

THE OLDEST KNOWN FOOTBALL PROGRAMME dates back to the 1893–94 season, the second year of League football, which suggests that the idea of a printed sheet bearing the players' names was probably introduced at the same time as organised football began.

Today the match day programme is a glossy production filled with all manner of information, some of it useful. Its value is really as a souvenir, which is why people are still prepared to pay for them, even though, in some cases, prices have trebled in the last 10 years. Their value to collectors is even greater, some rarities fetching several thousand pounds apiece.

In the 1980s, an era of great upheaval in the traditional running of football, many fans became disenchanted with the match programme and the lack of thought-provoking content within its pages, and turned instead to fanzines. Football fanzines were irreverent, amateur publications, put together by the fans for the fans. They spoke out on contentious issues and succeeded in galvanising supporters into organised movements against unpopular issues such as identity cards, racism and the various activities of club chairmen.

But the calming years of the 1990s placated many fans' anger and the match programme – bigger, shinier, and pricier than before – carried on regardless.

Left: A Southampton supporter outside the club's old stadium, The Dell, sells match programmes for the match against Tottenham on September 19, 1998

Far left: A Chelsea programme-seller outside Stamford Bridge in February 1949. Programmes from this era are valuable collectors' items today

1957

Good luck charm

MASCOTS HAVE A PART TO PLAY in any activity which counts on the blessing of Lady Luck. Army units, theatrical companies... and football teams. Traditionally, these mascots have been animals, usually dogs, which might be got up in the colours of whichever company they represent and paraded on ceremonial occasions.

The idea of the human mascot was most famously pioneered by Kenneth Bailey, who took it upon himself to become a mascot for England at every international sporting occasion. Dressed up like John Bull, he paraded around the ground waving the Union Jack and generally making a spectacle of himself. He died in 1993.

But by this time the football mascot had gone through an alarming transformation: now it was part man, part animal. Suddenly legions of ordinary everyday people were dressing up as oversized animals that represented some part of their club's tradition, like Pete the Eagle at Crystal Palace – by day headmaster of a London school, Pete the Eagle even starred in a TV commercial and immediately every club wanted a mascot like him.

Today, the fraternity of football mascots are an eccentric cornerstone of the game and each year they have their own Grand National, to find Britain's mascot champion.

Above: Chaddy Owl, the pride of Oldham Athletic, canters to victory in the 2002 Mascot Grand National at Huntingdon, ahead of a strong field of fake fur

Left: Dressing up in animal costumes is nothing new. Here the Millwall lion runs the gauntlet of fans at a match against Birmingham in February, 1957

Mr chairman

SUGAR DADDIES ARE NOTHING NEW IN FOOTBALL. Manchester United were twice saved from financial ruin, in 1902 and 1932, and in recent years clubs like Blackburn and Fulham have risen up the leagues thanks to the bankrolling of one man. The typical football chairman was a wealthy local businessman dressed appropriately in suit and bowler hat, who tended to stay in the background, keep hold of the purse strings and occasionally fire the manager. Today, club chairmen are fast becoming as much a part of the club's public image as the players themselves. They mingle with the supporters on foreign trips, parade around the pitch in the team colours and go on television or radio at the drop of a hat. In short, they are keen to be seen as fans first and foremost – but few supporters are prepared to buy that.

Too many chairmen have acted outside the best interests of their club for fans to regard them as one of their own. No matter how much money they pump into the transfer budget and the stadium renovation scheme, business will always be seen as their primary interest. It's one of those fundamental divisions that defines the structure of the game.

Left: April 28, 2001: Fulham chairman Mohammed Al Fayed, who owns Harrods, holds the First Division Champions trophy after a 1–1 draw with Wimbledon clinched the title for his club

Far left: Tottenham Hotspur chairman MF Cadman poses for a photograph after emerging from the FA headquarters at Lancaster Gate, London, on February 23, 1936

I V
JOINED
THE
RUDDY
POOL

1968

Razzmatazz

ATMOSPHERE IS A NEBULOUS THING and very difficult to generate artificially, but that doesn't stop people from trying. Traditionally fans created their own atmosphere simply through understanding the importance of each game, who the opposition were, how to wind them up etc. When entertainers appeared on the pitch before the game or at half-time, it was to join in rather than to take centre stage.

When all-seater stadiums replaced the terraces, however, the unique atmosphere of the football match dissolved. In an attempt to regenerate some of that old fervour for the new audience that was flocking to the game, entertainment was laid on to fill those times when supporters would have previously read the programme, had a hot drink or got an anthem going. From dancing troupes to chart-topping bands, the entertainers came and went, failing to meet their objective. The fans knew it had nothing to do with football.

The most spectacular failure of the entertainment world to capture football came in the opening ceremony of the 1994 World Cup in – where else – the USA. Diana Ross ran from the halfway line to crown her routine with a penalty shot into a theatrical goal from five yards. She missed.

Left: Actor Warren Mitchell, in the character of Alf Garnett from his TV sitcom *Till Death Us Do Part*, entertains the West Ham fans at Upton Park in February, 1968

Right: American singer Diana Ross gives it her all, shortly before her legendary penalty miss during the opening ceremony of the 1994 World Cup in the USA

Police presence

EVEN FOR THE LAW-ABIDING FANS, the sight of the police at the match has always had a comical edge to it. It became traditional, upon seeing the police move into position five minutes from the final whistle, to prevent fans from running on the pitch, for whole ends to start whistling the theme tune from the *Keystone Kops*. For those at the front, however, it wasn't so funny because the tall helmets could obliterate almost their entire view of the game.

Forced to stand facing the crowd rather than the action on the pitch, the police found themselves subjected to a torrent of abuse from fans, who clearly felt that the match, unlike real life outside the ground, was a place where they could vent spleen against anything that stood in their way.

But this was the more visible side of the force. As time moved on, the really serious police work at football went unnoticed. Undercover officers infiltrated hooligan gangs by pretending to be members, while closed-circuit cameras scoured the crowd for signs of trouble or notorious faces. As this type of surveillance began to make an impact, the numbers of visible police at the match decreased markedly.

Right: Police, together with a St John ambulanceman, try to keep warm as they watch the action in the snow at White Hart Lane in 1963

Far right: May 1, 1999: police move in to protect linesman Paul Norman at Upton Park after three West Ham players were sent off in a 5–1 defeat by Leeds

POLICE
POLICE
side

1949

Keeping the peace

RIGHT FROM THE EARLY YEARS of League football, the police have had a serious role to play keeping the peace at matches. Violence amongst fans was prevalent until the inter-war years, when the game gained a greater degree of respectability. In the 1960s, though, the rise in youth culture spawned new gangs, who took to football as a natural backdrop for their tribal warfare.

Such troubles have always been worst between rival fans from the same cities, such as Celtic and Rangers in Glasgow, whose mutual antipathy is exacerbated by sectarian differences. Meetings between these clubs have always called for a watchful police presence.

With so many years of practice, the British police became expert at controlling crowd trouble within the grounds and the gangs who wanted to pursue their violent vendettas were forced to find other battlegrounds. However, international matches still attract a violent element, fuelled by patriotism and the desire to 'fight for your country'. At the 2002 World Cup, Korean and Japanese police were ready for the worst. Vast ranks of riot police turned up for duty, almost outnumbering the fans. With the World sensitive to the threat of terrorism in the wake of September 11, there was good reason not to scrimp on security, but the much-feared hooligans never showed up.

Right: October 9, 1949: massed crowds at the Old Firm derby between Celtic and Rangers, a traditionally hostile affair, are kept in check by a couple of bobbies

Far right: Seogwipo, June 6, 2002. Korean police turn out in full riot gear for the World Cup Group B match between Slovenia and Paraguay

경 찰
POLICE

1931

The man in, er...

WHEN IT COMES TO THE SUPPORTING CAST, one man stands out above all else. They used to call him 'the man in black' (among other things) but now it's best to say 'the man in the middle'. Or, to be more straightforward, the referee. Despite what many managers have said just after a defeat, any referee is better than no referee at all and fortunately this is something they learned early on in the evolution of the game.

To distinguish them from the players, referees were dressed in black jacket and trousers that stopped just short of their ankles – an extraordinary sight that can't have helped in establishing respect for these amateurs in the professional game. In an effort to address the chronic lack of respect for football referees in comparison with, say, their rugby counterparts, some key changes have taken place.

Many of today's referees are full-time professionals and they are all expected to be much more on a par with the players, wearing the same kind of kit (although black is becoming less common) and striving for similar levels of fitness and athleticism. However, one golden rule still applies: never be tempted to try any ball skills. You will only fall flat on your face.

Left: November 21, 1931: Amateur referee E Weeks models the typical garb (though not necessarily the typical posture) of a football referee of the time

Right: September 1, 1999: the extraordinary Italian referee Pierluigi Collina, arguably the most respected official in the game, pulls one of those 'Don't mess with me' faces before Republic of Ireland versus Yugoslavia

1937

On camera

NOT SURPRISINGLY, FOOTBALLERS' relationship with the cameras took some time to reach the easy state of today. The Arsenal players filmed live in 1937 look like tribesmen from a lost civilisation as they peer into the lens, perhaps concerned that this contraption will steal their souls.

But once television got the go-ahead to broadcast League matches live on a regular basis in 1983, players quickly had to get used to the fact that their every move was being recorded. Up until then the emphasis had been on highlights shows, like *Match of the Day*, which first broadcast on August 22, 1964, and, in the interests of portraying the game in the best possible light, the most unseemly incidents tended to be edited out. The live format showed – up close and personal – exactly what players got up to and TV executives made it a priority to get closer and closer to the action. Cameras were mounted in the goals and hand-held steadicams were deployed at pitchside, offering a dynamic close-up of players at their own level.

The arrival of digital television expanded the options further still, allowing viewers to choose which camera view they wanted, and now the players go about their business barely noticing the cameras constantly following them. And as football increasingly dances to the programme-makers' tune, some people maintain that the game has indeed lost its soul.

Above: Steve Corica of Wolves gets treatment against Port Vale in April 1997, under the unflinching gaze of a steadicam, a revolutionary piece of TV equipment

Left: September 16, 1937, sees the first match to be screened live on television, Arsenal v Arsenal Reserves – not one for the neutral perhaps

1957

Authority figure

SO WHY ARE FOOTBALL REFEREES treated with so little respect? The arguments are many. Football is a passionate game and the referee is the scapegoat for all that emotion. Football is also a working-class game and, therefore, subservience to and respect for authority are not a part of it. Make of these what you will, but somewhere in the distant past football referees got off on the wrong foot, failed to stamp their authority on the game and have been paying for it ever since. Like it or not (and nobody will admit that they do), having a go at the ref is an ingrained part of football culture, for players, managers and fans alike.

For their part, referees are often criticised for behaving like schoolmasters, treating the players like children. But, as with teachers, occasionally a referee emerges who, for some indefinable reason, commands respect. He has charisma, maybe he frightens people, but he gets the job done and everybody admires him for that. If you could bottle it, it would fetch a handsome price. One thing, however, is easy to grasp. Referees improve with age. Once they are past the stage of having to establish themselves, they tend to use their own common sense and character and that invariably works better than the letter of the law.

Left: The referee admonishes the crowd for throwing fireworks at a match between Arsenal and Manchester City at Highbury on November 2, 1957

Right: Referee Graham Barber stands his ground as West Ham striker Paolo di Canio remonstrates with him over the dismissal of Marc-Vivien Foe in a match against Leeds at Upton Park on May 14, 2000

1937

The magic sponge

THE MAN RESPONSIBLE FOR THE WELLBEING of the players used to be called the trainer. He worked on their fitness and also administered first aid on the field of play. For this purpose his tools were a bucket of water and a sponge. An intricate medical science it was not. The technique was to douse the wounded area with freezing cold water, so that it either numbed the pain or made the player so reluctant to receive a second dose that he battled through the pain and got back to his feet. The trainer's medical bag expanded over the years to include smelling salts, the odd bandage and a pair of scissors. But even well into the 1990s there was a conspicuous absence of medical certificates. By then the trainer had become known as the physio, despite the fact that many had no physiotherapy qualifications.

Finally clubs started to realise that, if they were going to spend millions on players, it was worth investing a few quid in properly trained medical staff to look after them. The modern-day physio resembles a paramedic, sprinting on to the pitch in surgical gloves, carrying a bulging bag of medical supplies and a walkie-talkie, with which to relay details of the injury back to the bench.

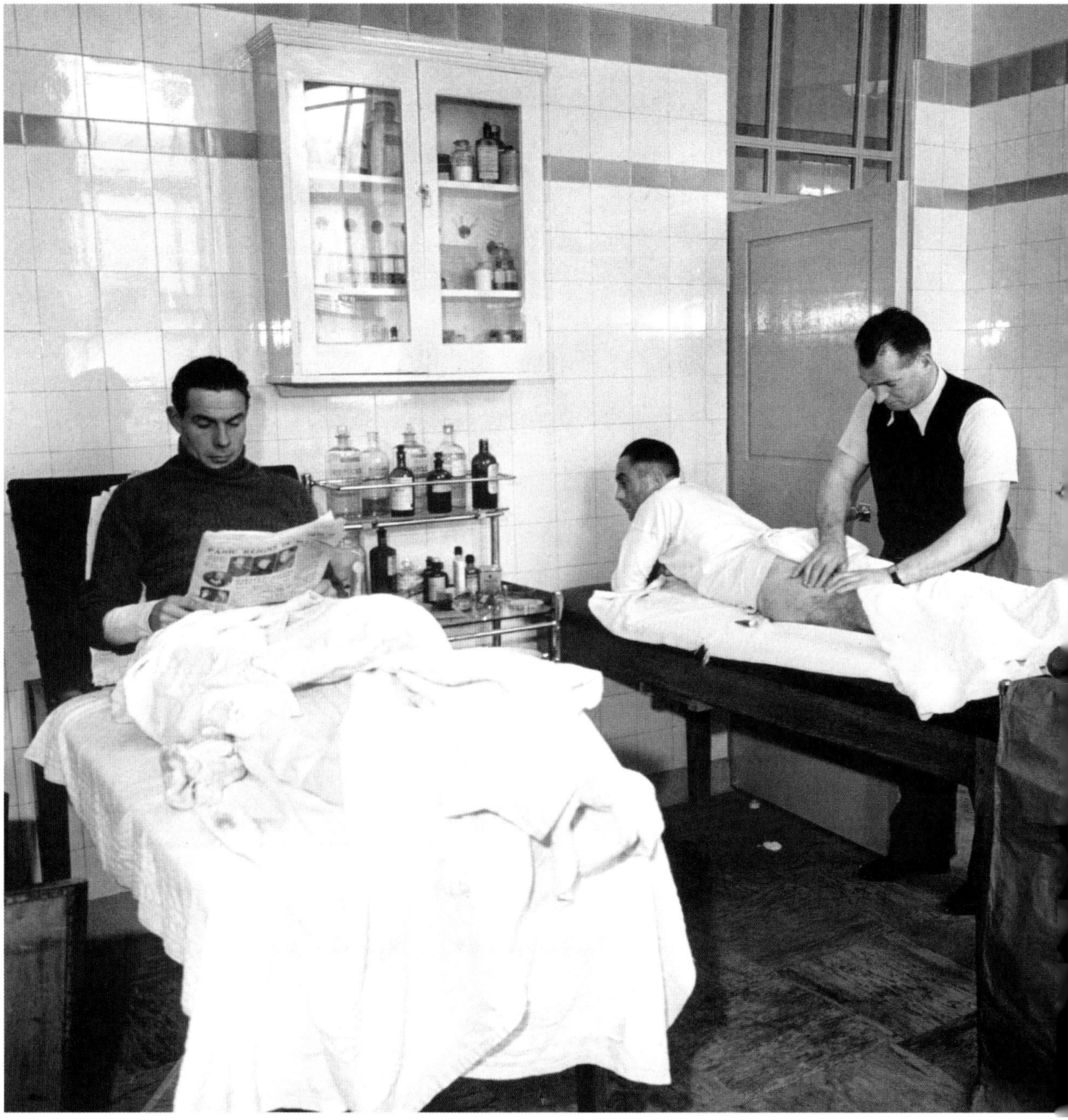

Left: Millwall centre-forward K Burditt receives some low-tech treatment from club trainer F Jeffries during a training session at The Den on March 2, 1937

Right: Arsenal physio Gary Lewin, complete with surgical gloves and walkie-talkie, relays information to the bench during the 2002 FA Cup semi-final against Middlesbrough at Old Trafford

Press box

AS THE MEDIA HAVE BECOME MORE AND MORE influential in football, so the facilities demanded by journalists and television reporters have become increasingly sophisticated. The traditional press box was a cramped affair, distinguished from the rest of the stand only by the writing tables and telephone and electricity sockets. When a key incident took place, the hacks would enquire amongst themselves as to which player did what, forming a consensus of opinion that passed into record, regardless of whether it was correct or not. Hence the common supporters' grumble when reading the reports: "He must have been watching a different game from me."

The modern press box offers plenty of elbow room and TV monitors, giving every opportunity for the commentators and reporters to get their facts right. Probably the most significant consequence is that every key incident is now studied in minute detail and poor decisions by the referee or his assistants become the source of much outrage. Of course, television pictures are often inconclusive, but that doesn't stop many figures in the media calling for television evidence to be used during matches to actually get the decisions right – thus perpetuating their own importance.

Right: From a cramped position, with several obstacles in the way, Douglas Remfrey (mic) and his brother Bill try to commentate on a match in 1956 for hospital radio

Far right: June 25, 1998: televisions on every desk help the media to follow the World Cup group F game between Yugoslavia and the USA in Nantes, France

107
L'EQUIPE

1973

Media pressure

FOOTBALL MANAGERS HAVE TO BE GOOD at relationships. First, they have to strike up a good relationship with their chairman. That gets them the job. Next, they have to forge a strong working relationship with their staff and players. That gets the job done. Finally, and perhaps most importantly, they have to establish a relationship with the press. That can keep them in the job. Or it can see them booted out.

It wasn't ever thus. The Managerial Merry-go-round – a phrase coined by the press – was something that didn't really get going until the 1970s, when newspaper editors caught up in a circulation war realised that intrigue and speculation over a football manager's future made good copy. Until then, the relationship between managers and the press had been mostly affable, sometimes even close. The small body of journalists, many of them ex-players, who followed the teams around were regarded as part of the game and welcomed into the fold. But once the news hounds got in on the act, it all turned sour. Managers became twitchy, paranoid even, and that just made the stories more compelling.

Today, the media scrum that follows football is something managers endure rather than enjoy, remembering all the time that, without the media, their job (while they have it) wouldn't be worth a fraction of the salary it is.

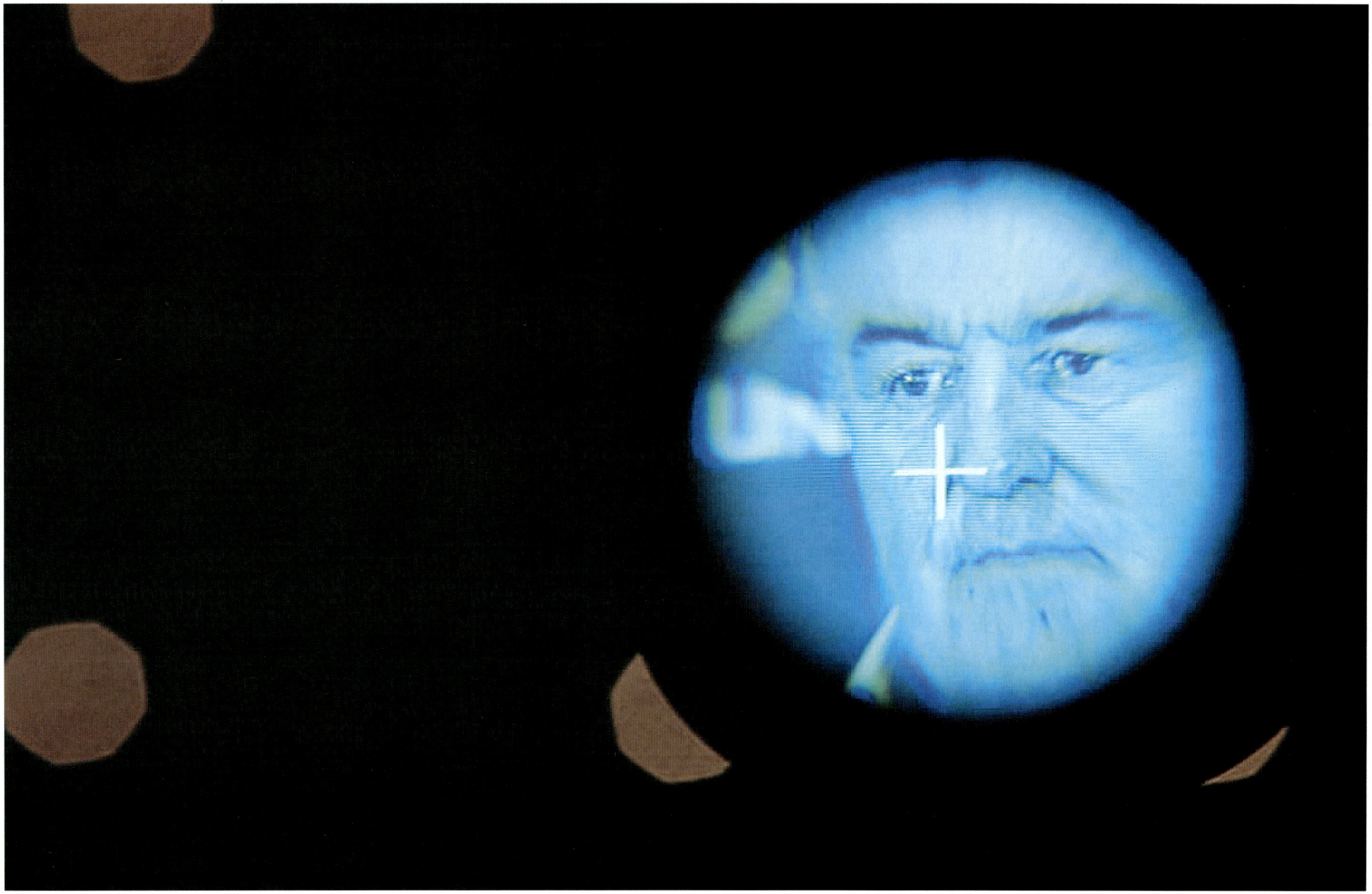

Above: The target of intense media scrutiny, Terry Venables is caught on camera as he is unveiled as Leeds' new manager in July 2002. A few months later he was gone...

Left: September 17, 1973: West Ham manager Ron Greenwood, later to manage England, makes a statement to obedient journalists over the future of club captain Bobby Moore

Five:

Objects of desire

Right: The boot room at Highbury in December 1951, which has since transferred to the training ground at London Colney and its footwear has burst into colour

1935

Object of the exercise

THE ORIGINS OF THE FOOTBALL are shrouded in myth and legend. We all know about the inflated pig's bladder that got booted from one end of the village to the other by our ancestors, but in some cultures it's said they used to play with the heads of vanquished warriors. Difficult to float a through-ball into the path of your striker, one would have thought, but who knows? Those were savage times.

When organised football began in the 19th Century, the make-up of the ball became governed by regulations. The Laws of the Game state that the ball must be spherical with a circumference of 68-71cm and must weigh between 396g and 453g at the start of the game. This final point was made because the old leather balls could double in weight when they soaked up water.

The natural brown of the leather was the standard colour until the 1950s, when the introduction of floodlit football led to white balls being used. Today, ball manufacturers invest heavily in technology, fine-tuning the amount of power, swerve etc a player can exercise to the nth degree. But one fact remains true: if the person shooting can't kick straight, it ain't going to go in.

Above: Adidas won the contract to supply the official match ball for the 2002 World Cup in South Korea and Japan and came up with this, the FeverNova

Left: 1935: Two boys wait in eager anticipation as their older brother does his best to inflate a leather football, complete with lace

These colours don't run

TODAY A CLUB'S COLOURS ARE AN UNSHAKEABLE part of its identity and changing them is unthinkable. But for many years clubs and countries experimented with different strips. Even as late as the 1960s, Leeds United played in blue and gold, changing to all-white in a bid by manager Don Revie to emulate the great Real Madrid. These days, clubs are still able to exercise their creative imagination by re-colouring their change strip on a regular basis. Indeed, the relaxation in rules governing the colours of shirts has led to some extraordinary designs that would have looked smart on a beach towel or shower curtain but had no rightful place on a football field.

The job of washing all this kit has got a lot easier with the introduction of man-made materials in place of the old cotton shirts. Not only are they much lighter for the players to wear, they also dry a lot more quickly, saving on laundry time. The latest shirt designs involve two layers in order to keep the player warm, while still allowing the skin to breathe. The only trouble is, once a player has taken his shirt off to celebrate a goal, it can take up to five minutes to get it back on again.

Right: August 14, 1935: on the eve of the new season, Tottenham's laundress hangs out the first-team and reserve kit on the White Hart Lane washing line

Far right: A Nigerian team's football shirts, held down by stones, dry on a wall in the sun during the African Nations Cup in February 2000

1939

Shirt numbers

IT WASN'T UNTIL 1939, just as League football was about to take a six-year break for World War II, that the Football League approved the numbering of players' shirts. Up until then, some pioneering managers like Herbert Chapman at Arsenal had experimented with it, but in most cases you had to identify players by looks alone. The numbering in those days was quite straightforward: 1=goalkeeper, 2 and 3=full-backs etc. The most charismatic number was 9 – the centre-forward – and the term 'big number 9' became part of everyday football vocabulary.

By the 1990s, the merchandisers had come to realise you could sell more shirts if they represented certain players, so shirts started to carry the players' names as well as numbers. But what if a player was dropped one week and somebody else had to wear the number 7? The solution was quickly found. Give every player a squad number, which they stick to throughout the season. That way, the souvenir shops could carry replicas with Beckham 7, Keane 16 etc without having to change. The downside, of course, was that the players on the field, instead of being numbered 1 to 9, were numbered 1, 16, 24, 232...

Left: New Year, 1939, and Tottenham players Hall A., Hall W. and Duncan study their new numbered shirts, trying to figure out if it's a 9 or a 6

Right: Numbers aren't enough these days, the shirts have names too. Ronaldo lines up for Internazionale against Lazio in the 1998 UEFA Cup Final at the Parc des Princes, Paris

RONALDO
10

Footwear

IF YOU WERE TO BELIEVE the marketing spiel of football boot manufacturers, you would think it impossible to play the game beyond the level of an idiot without having the right footwear. What it really boils down to, of course, is finding a piece of leather that fits your foot comfortably, so you can run and kick and dribble without feeling like you've got a heavy fruitcake moulded round your toes. In this respect, football boots have evolved almost beyond recognition.

Whereas the early football boots were designed to afford maximum protection from lunging tackles, today their purpose is more akin to ballet shoes: light, comfortable and supple enough for the subtle movements of the foot to translate to the ball, without being baffled by half an inch of cow on the way.

You could say, then, that the Nigerian team that visited England in 1950 was ahead of its time, choosing to play without boots at all. Their ball control was a delight to watch, until a burly defender from Bishop Auckland brought his hobnails down on their metatarsals.

Until the 1990s, wearing coloured boots was guaranteed to bring you into ridicule, but now is the age of the fancy Dan.

Right: A Nigerian side touring England in 1950 display their preference for playing barefoot as they prepare to take on Bishop Auckland in toeless socks and shinpads

Far right: Manchester United v Middlesbrough, 2002: the focus is on David Beckham's new boots, embroidered with the names of his sons Brooklyn and Romeo

Romeo
Brooklyn

GREENGROCER
NED'S
FRUITERER
GREAT TEAM
CUP FINAL
1970
BIRDS EYE
shop
OR LOSE
UP THE

1978

Getting the message across

FANS MAY BE THE SPECTATORS while players hog the limelight, but when the occasion demands the stands and terraces can be a commanding stage from which to get your message across. Football supporters have never been backward in coming forward, whether celebrating their team's success or campaigning against hardship, and the history of the game is decorated with home-made props designed to draw attention to the crowd.

The FA Cup final can send participating fans into a frenzy of prop-making and banner-painting. In 1987, a Coventry fan, delirious at reaching the Cup Final for the first time ever, spent an hour painting a huge banner on his mum's living room floor, only to lift it up and find his words of wisdom had soaked through to the carpet. Huge rosettes and silly hats are a safer bet.

In the 1980s, there was a brief but glorious trend for inflatables, sparked by the appearance of blow-up bananas at Manchester City. During an FA Cup-tie between Wimbledon and Grimsby, the away end at Plough Lane was transformed into a sea of inflatable haddock as the Mariners took the lead.

Left: Staff at a grocer's shop in World's End, west London, grab whatever comes to hand as they prepare to cheer Chelsea to victory in the FA Cup in 1970

Right: Selhurst Park, August 24, 2002: Brighton fans come out in sympathy with the plight of their Wimbledon counterparts, as the Dons get ready to relocate to Milton Keynes under orders from the board of directors

1974

Card play

UNDER THE LAWS OF THE GAME, there are seven offences for which a player can be sent off the field of play: 1, serious foul play; 2, violent conduct; 3, spitting at another person; 4, deliberate handball to prevent a goal; 5, fouling an opponent to deny a clear goalscoring opportunity; 6, using offensive, insulting or abusive language or gestures; 7, receiving a second booking. Since the introduction of number 5 – the professional foul – the number of red cards has greatly increased.

Indeed, up until 1976 there were no red cards at all. That is not to say there were no dismissals, but the showing of red and yellow cards to signify sendings-off and bookings was only introduced in that year. Before that, referees informed players that their early bath was ready with a dismissive wave of the hand or a quiet word in the ear: "You're off!"

The use of cards was suspended again in 1981 because this overt display of punishment was considered inflammatory in an era when fans needed little provocation to cause trouble. But it was reintroduced again in 1987 by popular demand, since when referees have worked hard on their card-brandishing technique, in order to exact maximum drama from the moment.

Left: Referee R Matthenson sends off Billy Bremner of Leeds (left) and Liverpool's Kevin Keegan after the pair traded punches during the 1974 Charity Shield match at Wembley

Right: Mexican referee A Brizo shows the red card to Bolivia's Marco Etcheverry in a match against Germany during the 1994 World Cup in Chicago, USA

1956

The wall

A DIRECT FREE-KICK within shooting range is a potent weapon for any team that has worked hard on its set-pieces. You have the option to work a clever move, float the ball on to the head of your tallest players or shoot for goal. It's to prevent the latter that the wall was first thought up. There's nothing complicated about the defensive wall: you just line up a few men 10 yards from the kick to cover the angles to goal. If properly positioned, the only way to shoot the ball past the wall is over the top.

And that's where the free-kick specialist comes in. At the sort of distances in question, the laws of physics dictate that a straightforward kick over the wall will send the ball several feet over the crossbar. You need to put considerable spin on the ball to bring it down, a skill that requires endless practice. In 1956, a German engineer called Josef Patcha designed an artificial wall for just this purpose. Made of inflatable cylinders with concrete bases, it presented a life-size obstacle that moved realistically in the wind. Practice makes perfect, but even world-class, dead-ball experts such as Robert Prosinecki of Croatia find it impossible to hit the target every time.

Right: 1956: German engineer Josef Patcha stands in goal while his son prepares to try a free-kick against his newly invented 'wall', made out of inflatable cylinders

Far right: June 3, 2002: Croatia's Robert Prosinecki sends a free-kick over the Mexican wall at the Niigata stadium but fails to score. Mexico won the game 1–0

ROSINECKI

1966

Refreshment

THE DEVELOPMENT OF THE FOOTBALL player as an athlete has involved a revolution in terms of what they put in their bodies. Where once you had a drink because you were thirsty, now you 're-hydrate' because your body needs those vital minerals, and fizzy water is discouraged. Re-hydration has become a science that all players are aware of and, in most cases, they can be trusted to ensure they take good care of themselves in this respect.

It used to be the norm to come in at half-time and have a cup of tea. A lovely, thirst-quenching brew with a good dollop of sugar in it to get you going again. But dieticians discovered that tea would actually drain your energies, rather than enhance them. World Cup tournaments in places like Mexico and the USA forced managers to think very seriously about re-hydration, to get their players through 90 minutes in fierce heat. Bags of water thrown to players on the pitch became a feature of the USA 94 tournament and now part of the kit man's duties is to lay out a row of water bottles along the touchline. No longer are players forced to wait for their turn at the hot water bottle, like Eusebio in 1966.

Left: During the World Cup third/fourth play-off between Portugal and Russia in 1966, Eusebio refuels from a hot water bottle as he leads Portugal to a 2–1 victory

Right: Arsenal and Sweden forward Freddie Ljungberg takes on water in the heat of Kobe, Japan, during his country's 2–1 World Cup win over Nigeria in 2002

Carried off

OH DEAR! IF EVER THERE WAS A FEELING that modern players are pampered compared to their predecessors, these pictures would appear to prove it. Injury is the hard side to the game and for players whose livelihood depends on staying fit, it hasn't got any easier. But the treatment of injured players has.

In the days before 1965, when substitutes were allowed for the first time, being stretchered off meant you had to be on the brink of death. If you could still breathe, you were expected to play on, rather than leave your team a man short. Treatment consisted of a dousing with the magic sponge.

The use of a buggy to carry injured players off the field was first seen at the 1994 World Cup in the USA. A measure designed to stop time-wasting by players feigning injury, it worked up to a point, inasmuch as most players were too embarrassed to accept a lift on the 'milk float', as Emile Heskey's facial expression shows in this picture. However, by the time the buggy had trundled its way out on to the pitch, picked up its cargo and then trundled off again, the game had usually lost its flow. Perhaps buggies should have stayed on the golf course where they belong.

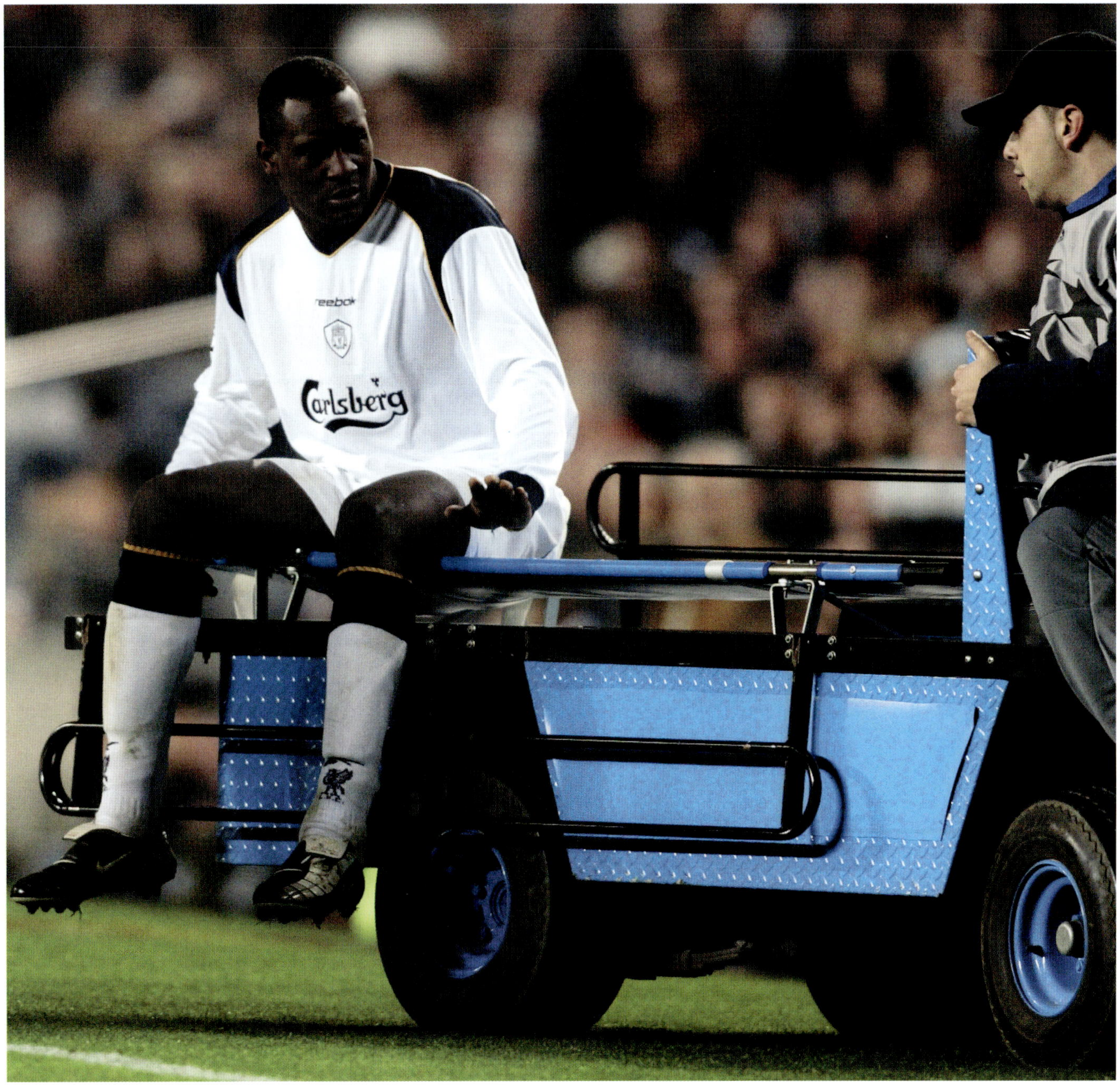

Left: Don't worry, it's only a prank. In the 1936 Jockeys v Boxers match, fighter Dave Crowley plays along with the Crazy Gang for the amusement of the crowd

Right: Clearly not proud of this particular mode of transport, Liverpool's Emile Heskey sits awkwardly on the injury cart during his side's 2002 Champions League match against Barcelona

1933

Time pieces

TIME IS THE ENEMY OF EVERY LOSING SIDE and tension increases as the clock counts down to the final whistle. Many fans prefer not to wear a watch to the match for this very reason. And players are best advised not to worry about the time but to concentrate on the job in hand until the whistle blows. Kenny Dalglish's memorable 'one minute' signal to Steve McMahon in 1989, just before Michael Thomas scored for Arsenal to snatch the title from Liverpool in the dying seconds, is a case in point.

Possibly for this reason, many stadiums did without clocks, Arsenal's being a famous exception, but with the advent of electronic scoreboards came an increased focus on time. Today it's hard to avoid the time at the match, with many scoreboards counting down the minutes from the kick-off.

In the late 1990s it was deemed from on high that everybody actually needed to know exactly how much time there was remaining and the amount of injury time to be played was signalled around the ground on an electronic board held up by the fourth official. Of course, if you don't want to know you can always look away, but there's bound to be some clown nearby who blurts out, "Four minutes!"

Right: December 4, 1933: the famous Highbury clock shows twenty-five past two as Arsenal play a friendly against First Vienna from Austria

Far right: The fourth official, Anders Frisk, holds up the indicator board just before extra time between China and Costa Rica in their 2002 World Cup Group C match at the Gwangju Stadium, South Korea

FIFAworldcup.com
Gillette
adidas
Yahoo!

What's the score?

IT'S NOT OFTEN THAT THE CROWD need reminding of the score in a game but it's rare these days to visit a ground that doesn't tell you. Before the development of electronic scoreboards, you might have got a board with painted numbers hung up if you were lucky, but generally it was assumed that even the dullest fan could keep the score in his head. After all, we're not talking about cricket. So why are scoreboards so popular now? Well, it's probably a consequence of advertising.

Electronic scoreboards were mainly installed to convey messages to the supporters about forthcoming games, ticket sales, fans' birthdays etc, and when they did show the score it was often unreliable: 7–0 just meant that one of the zeros wasn't working properly. The incentive to relay bigger and brighter messages brought about the use of jumbo screens and, since they were there and they weren't allowed to show action replays while play was going on, well, they might as well show the score. In some instances it becomes an act of sheer antagonism; nobody likes to be reminded when they're losing 3–1.

Right: A scoreboard set up at White City for spectators of the Varsity Sports on March 9, 1932, to show the scores in the FA Cup semi-finals taking place the same day

Far right: The scoreboard at the Philips Stadium in Eindhoven shows the result of the Champions League match between Dutch club PSV and Manchester United in September, 2000

Philips Stadion
PSV
Man. Utd
3
90:00
1

K·CW·920G

1972

Chariots of fire

BEFORE THE ABOLITION of the maximum wage in 1961, top footballers in Britain earned £20 a week during the season, less in the close season. Compare that to the £20,000 a week picked up by the average Premiership player four decades on and you get a clear illustration of how the status of footballers has soared in terms of personal wealth. If inflation had risen at the same rate (one hundred thousand per cent), a pint of beer would now cost £100.

Even after the maximum wage had been removed, it took some time for most players to begin to earn big money. When England won the World Cup in 1966, they received £22,000 between them – £1,000 for each member of the squad. A footballer's earning power was equivalent to that of a bank clerk and, if you turned up to training in a Rover, you'd attract envious glances from your teammates.

Today, footballers become millionaires in a few short seasons and the training ground car parks are full of the sort of marques that even George Best could only dream of in the 1960s. Well, they've got to spend all that money on something.

Left: April 24, 1972: Manchester City star Francis Lee relaxes on the bonnet of his Jag, his obvious pride and joy, outside City's Maine Road ground

Right: Italy and Roma star Francesco Totti pauses to sign a few autographs as he leaves his club's Trigoria training ground, safely ensconced behind the wheel of his massive Ferrari in the year 2000

Six:

When the whistle blows

Right: Brazilian players are unhappy about a penalty given against them at Wembley in 1956. In the end, the spot kick was missed but England still won 4–2

5

1931

Fly-past

EVER SINCE MAN FIRST TOOK TO THE SKIES, major football events have been used as a good excuse for a fly-past. In 1996, spectators at the final of the African Nations Cup in Johannesburg, South Africa, were treated to the sight of a low-flying jumbo jet, creating this spectacular photograph. Somehow the great bulk of the jet reflects the enormity of the event. This was the first Cup of Nations to be held in South Africa since the end of Apartheid and the lifting of sporting sanctions, as well as the first time the South Africa team, or *Bafana Bafana*, had been allowed to enter. Amazingly, they went on to beat Tunisia 2–0 in the final.

But back in 1931 an altogether more ominous sight greeted the spectators at Wembley Stadium for the FA Cup Final. The huge German airship, *Graf Zeppelin*, hovered low over rain-soaked north-west London, looming slowly into view like a harbinger of doom. Although the 776-foot blimp was a popular sight around the world, it would soon be seen as an ominous symbol of Hitler's growing strength.

For cup finalists Birmingham City, it certainly proved an ill omen, as a dubiously disallowed goal cost them dear against local rivals West Bromwich Albion.

Above: The spectacular *Graf Zeppelin* airship establishes a tradition at Wembley, while West Bromwich Albion beat Birmingham 2–1 in the 1931 FA Cup Final

Right: A huge jumbo jet flies over the national stadium in Johannesburg to mark the historic occasion of South Africa's hosting of the African Nations Cup, 1996

Goalkick

ONE ASPECT OF THE GAME THAT HASN'T CHANGED over the years is the goalkick. The ball placed anywhere in the six-yard box and wellied upfield remains an integral part of the goalkeeper's weaponry... and a moment when he knows the whole ground is watching him.

Opposition fans usually take this opportunity to try to unnerve the keeper as he runs up to strike the ball, with a "Whoooooooooooooah!" building to a crescendo at the point of contact and, in latter years, an insulting chant. Most goalkeepers shrug it off, but any scuffed kick or slip of the standing foot makes it all worthwhile.

What's interesting about these two pictures, taken half a century apart, is the amount of heavy being put into the kick. Pat Bonner appears to have kicked the ball miles with a graceful swing of the right boot, while George Swindin has launched himself into the kick with every ounce of strength in his body. This is largely due to the density of the ball – leather versus plastic – although better technique has also improved kicking distances.

Today, a big kick isn't enough, though. The backpass rule has meant goalkeepers must have a good first touch allied to great volleying technique.

Right: A London derby between Chelsea and Arsenal at Stamford Bridge on February 10, 1937, and Arsenal keeper George Swindin clears his lines

Far right: Celtic and Republic of Ireland goalkeeper Pat Bonner kicks the ball into Dundee United territory during the 1988 Scottish Cup Final at Hampden Park

1955

Aerial combat

THE SET-PIECE HAS BECOME an increasing danger for defences, as coaches spend hours on the training ground working out new and cunning moves.

But in most cases the set-piece boils down to the same thing it always has: capitalising on aerial advantage. If you've got a man who is taller or can jump higher than anyone else on the pitch, all you've really got to do is float the ball accurately on to his head and the goals should rapidly follow.

The aerial ball has always played a big part in British football and the strategy of having big centre-forwards and big centre-halves, for the very purpose of both capitalising on and defending against the aerial ball, still runs through the game today. And coaches have yet to find a way of nullifying the threat of the big man who lumbers forward for set-pieces.

If your biggest man is not as big as their biggest man, you either have to rely on your goalkeeper to come and pluck the ball out of the air, or you gang up on their main threat, as Liverpool do here against Everton's Duncan Ferguson.

Left: Liverpool players, (l–r) Karl-Heinz Riedle, Steve Staunton and Jamie Carragher, take care of Everton's danger man Duncan Ferguson, aka The Walking Forehead, in a 4–2 win at Christmas 1998

Far left: December 12, 1955: Kalliztakis, goalkeeper of Greek second-division team Proodeftiki, leaps over team-mate Karponides (right) and Christofides of Panelefssiniakos

Putting yourself about

AS ANY PLAYER WILL REMIND YOU as they pick you up off the floor, football is a contact sport in which aggression plays a major role. If you can convince your opponent that you are tougher, stronger and, essentially, more likely to do damage than they are, you have the upper hand in any duel that may follow. This is grim reality for every player, but some take to the idea with exaggerated relish.

These are what we call the 'Hard Men' and they've existed in football since day one. In fact, if truth be told, the Hard Man has gradually dwindled in numbers as the game has evolved from the kicking matches of the 19th Century to the supposed artistry of the modern age. But those that remain still command respect or hatred, depending on whether they play for or against you.

They used to have nicknames, like Ron 'Chopper' Harris of Chelsea and Norman 'Bites Yer Legs' Hunter of Leeds, whereas today such affectionate sobriquets seem inappropriate for the likes of Roy 'Writes Nasty Things About You' Keane and Dennis 'Gets His Lawyers Onto You' Wise.

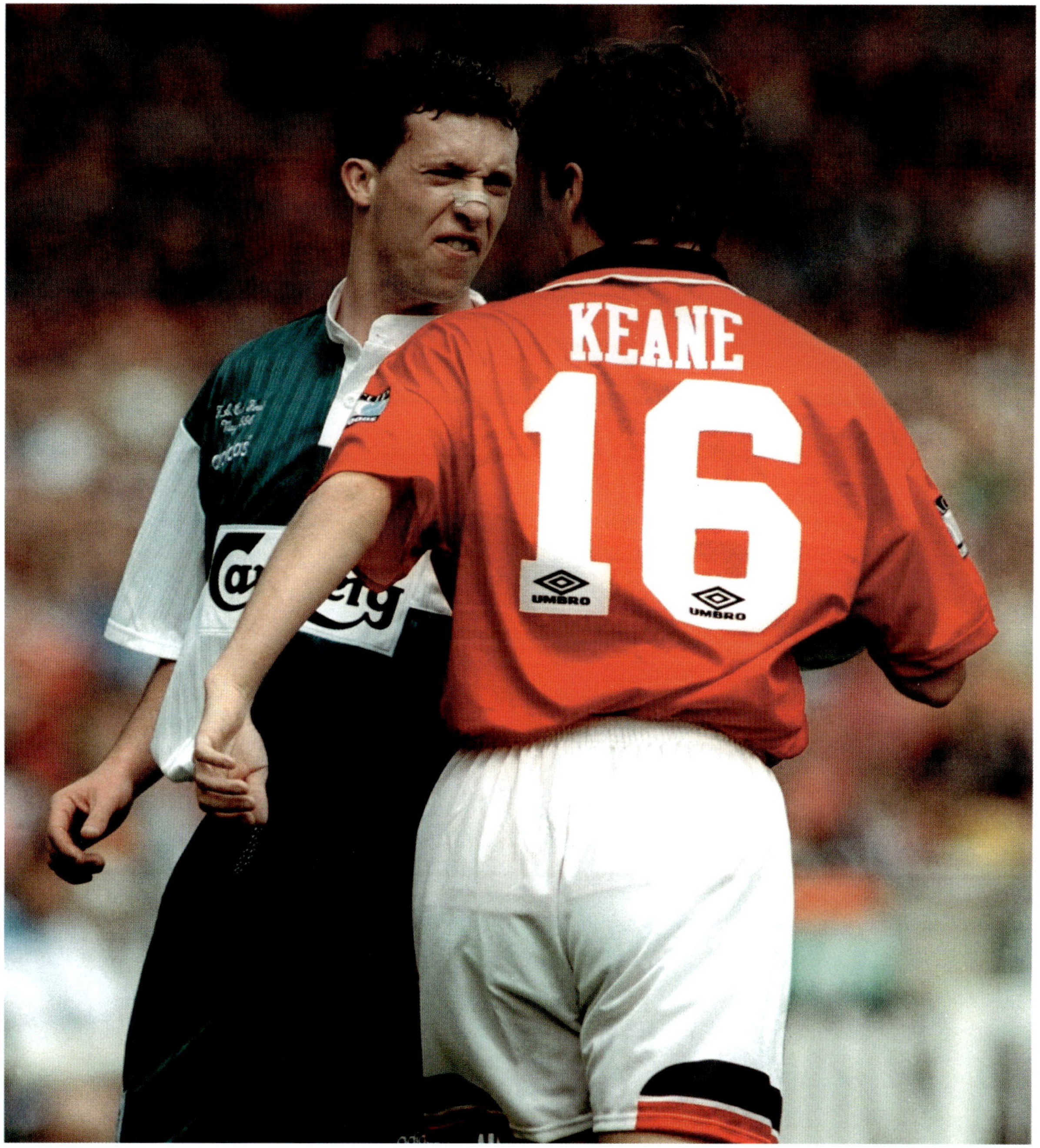

Left: Liverpool's Robbie Fowler offers a frank exchange of views with Manchester United hard man Roy Keane in the 1996 FA Cup Final, won 1–0 by United

Far left: February 23, 1974, and Chelsea full-back Ron 'Chopper' Harris – one of the most feared tacklers ever – brings down QPR's Stan Bowles in a match at Stamford Bridge

1970

Never the twain

ONE OF THE MAGICAL QUALITIES OF FOOTBALL is that its style and interpretation vary from country to country. By comparison with most footballing nations, the British style of play is quite restrained and unfussy – albeit quick – and that is generally the way the British in general are seen throughout the world. Similarly, in Italy the game is full of flamboyance and expression, in keeping with the stereotype of the Italian people.

While the British find much to admire in the Italian style of play and vice versa, the two are about as dissimilar as it is possible to get within the 12 Laws of the Game. The Italian style is a confusing combination of uncompromising hardness and flamboyant overacting – sometimes it's hard to tell when a player has dived and when he's actually been launched through the air.

The British style sits between the two extremes, in fear of Italian tackling, in contempt of the theatricals. The two styles have traditionally struggled to mix. The number of British players who have adapted successfully to Italian league football can be counted on the fingers of one hand, and the same applies the other way round.

Left: Inter Milan forward Pino Boninsegna manages to leap a scything tackle from Lazio's Giorgio Papadopulo during their match at the Olympic Stadium in Rome in 1970

Right: November 28, 1993: Italian midfielder Roberto Donadoni of AC Milan makes the most of a foul by Roberto Sensini of Parma during their Serie A match at the Ennio Tardini stadium

Flying save

THEY SAY THAT GOALKEEPER is the loneliest position on the field. For most of the game you are a mere spectator and yet you are regularly called upon to show bravery beyond anything your team-mates would dream of and everybody is quick to blame you for your mistakes.

However, goalkeeper is also the most spectacular position on the field. No other player gets the chance to fly through the air quite like a 'keeper and, because the photographers are nearly always positioned right behind you, your dashing exploits are bound to be caught on film.

These are just two examples from a huge selection of goalkeeping acrobatics. What is striking about them is the body position of the keepers featured, Harry Gregg and Erik Thorstvedt. The arched back, the outstretched arms, the eyes fixed on the ball and the legs bending backwards; anyone who has ever played 'Subbuteo' will immediately recognise the textbook 'diving save' position.

Mind you, a good dive doesn't always mean a good save. While Thorstvedt managed to parry his shot round the post, Gregg was helpless to stop this goal by Germany's Uwe Seeler.

Left: Northern Ireland and Manchester United goalkeeper Harry Gregg keeps his hat on but can't keep out a strike by Uwe Seeler in a 2–2 draw with West Germany in the 1958 World Cup in Malmo, Sweden

Right: Tottenham Hotspur's Norwegian goalkeeper Erik Thorstvedt stretches full length to tip away an Aston Villa shot in a League match on September 9, 1990

Handbags

VIOLENT CONDUCT IS, OF COURSE, a sending-off offence, but this ultimate deterrent is not always enough to keep players under control. In such a physical game, tempers inevitably boil over from time to time. That said, there are certain players you would never associate with violence on the field of play. Sir Bobby Charlton, who was never booked in his career, is a classic example. The same might be said of his great contemporary Pele... until you saw this picture.

It has to be said that Pele was more sinned against than sinner. In the 1966 World Cup he was mercilessly kicked by all his opponents until he couldn't go on. But at that time, Brazil had the worst disciplinary record in World Cup history. At the 1938 tournament, their game against Germany had seen three people sent off and, in 1954, they were involved in a mass brawl against Hungary, which was later dubbed the 'Battle of Berne'.

Vinnie Jones, on the other hand, was a player who was not unfamiliar with the referee's notebook. The former hod-carrier who made his name as the leader of Wimbledon's 'Crazy Gang' was sent off a dozen times in his career and set the record for the quickest-ever booking: five seconds after kick-off.

Left: An astonishing picture of Santos and Brazil legend Pele throwing a punch at Masiero of Internazionale as the two sides brawl in June, 1963

Right: Vinnie Jones of QPR gets a grip on fellow old-stager Steve Claridge of Wolves as the two clubs clash at Loftus Road on April Fool's Day, 1998

GOODYEAR
PUMA
ERICSSON
Nationwide

It never rains...

THE WEATHER ADDS AN EXTRA dimension to football, affecting both the playing surface and the conditions governing the movement of the ball. The direction of the wind, position of the sun (if there is any): all this has a bearing on the tactics of the game. With the season starting and ending in summer but passing through the depths of winter, the weather even affects the shape of a championship campaign. Some teams fare better on dry pitches, others like the rough and tumble of a rain-soaked affair.

One of the undeniable changes for the better has been the ability of groundstaff to cope with severe weather conditions and get the game on. Undersoil heating has become more widespread, putting an end to postponements enforced by frozen pitches. And special covers have helped to overcome the debilitating effects of snow.

While nostalgic fans may long for the days when the orange ball was unwrapped for a game in the snow, the reduction in postponements, especially around the FA Cup third round in January, is a great improvement. What's more, better pitches generally mean better football... but there's nothing wrong with a bit of grease on top. It livens any game up.

Right: Players try to keep their feet in several inches of snow during a midlands Football League match between unnamed teams in 1938 – note the rolled-up sleeves

Far right: Michael Owen of Liverpool and England gets caught in the rain during his country's 3–0 victory over Denmark in the 2002 World Cup in Niigata, Japan

OWEN
10

4

1966

Yeeeeeeeees!

GARY LINEKER ONCE DESCRIBED it as "better than sex". The feeling you get when you put the ball in the net is one of such exhilaration that it prompts the most extraordinary reaction. The spreading of the arms, the jump in the air, the lung-bursting roar of "Yeeeeeeeeeeees!" – when you look at it all in the cold light of day, it's quite alarming. Yet at the time it's completely natural.

Obviously some pretty powerful emotion is taking hold somewhere inside the brain. Goal celebrations have become part of the theatre of modern football, with players taking the opportunity to act out rehearsed routines, or to make some statement through a message on a T-shirt or a quick sniff of the goal line (stand up, Robbie Fowler). In the old days, goal celebrations were said to be more modest – a simple handshake, maybe one arm raised – but there were still plenty of players who couldn't stop themselves jumping for joy, often several times, with apparently no concept of what a Charlie they'd look to future generations. This shot of Geoff Hurst, however, is a textbook goal celebration, made to appear even more dramatic by the fact that he is leaping out of the top of the frame.

Left: Geoff Hurst jumps for joy after scoring the winner against Argentina in the 1966 World Cup quarter-final. Roger Hunt (left) and Alan Ball also show their delight

Right: September 1, 2001 and Michael Owen celebrates scoring for England in a 5–1 demolition of Germany in Munich. Sol Campbell runs to join in

That sinking feeling

GOAL! THE CROWNING MOMENT, the climax, the moment of unbounded joy... and despair. Never is the loneliness of the goalkeeper felt more acutely than when he's beaten. It's one thing that never changes. To turn in despair and see the ball dropping over you into an unguarded net is a feeling that only goalkeepers – and the occasional defender – have to endure.

The sense of loss is magnified by the roar of the opposition fans, insensitive to your pain, their delight accentuating your misery as you forlornly pick the ball out of the back of the net. What is cruellest of all, even the best goalkeepers, those who perform heroics, who win their team medals and honours through their genius, even they still have to go through this humiliating ritual on a regular basis.

When England keeper David Seaman was lobbed from a free-kick by Brazil's Ronaldinho, all his good work was forgotten. Thoughts went back to another famous lob, by Nayim of Real Zaragoza, which beat him from almost the halfway line in the Cup Winners' Cup final in 1995. And suddenly Seaman was a liability. That's the damage a goal can do. Who would be a keeper?

Left: It's that horrible sense of humiliation for the Juventus 'keeper as Brazilian Jair scores for Internazionale in an Italian Serie A match in 1962

Right: David Seaman turns in despair as Ronaldinho's free-kick catches him off his line to give Brazil victory over England in the quarter-final of the 2002 World Cup

JVC
Budweiser

In the net

GOAL-NETS WERE FIRST USED in an official capacity in 1891 during a match at the Old Etonians' ground in Liverpool. The following year they were used in the FA Cup Final. They were the invention of a man called JA Brodie, who patented the idea in 1890. But after their initial introduction it took a while to get the right tension in the mesh. When they were made too tight, there were cases of the ball pinging back out of the goal, unnoticed by the referee who assumed it had hit the woodwork and waved play on. Amazingly, the same thing happened as recently as 1970, causing Aston Villa to be relegated to Division Three.

There is still no universal standard goal-net used in football. Styles vary all over the world, from the fairly shallow but slack nets popular at British grounds, where there's little space around the pitch, to the taut, deep nets favoured in Spain and elsewhere.

Strikers don't seem to care which they are, as long as they hit them with some regularity. The sight of the ball being arrested in flight by the net is the trigger for football's greatest joy.

Left: David Johnson, then of Ipswich Town, follows the ball into the back of the net in a Home International against Wales at Wembley on May 21, 1975

Right: Arsenal's prolific goalscorer Ian Wright celebrates in typically flamboyant style after scoring in a 3–1 win over Southampton at Highbury on December 4, 1996

1947

How long to go?

KEEP GOING UNTIL THE FINAL WHISTLE. That's the old cliche, insisted on by every manager. But when will the final whistle come? It has become harder and harder to predict. The game is supposed to be played over 90 minutes, 45 minutes each way, and that is how it used to be – simple as that. But, like every law of the game, cynics hijacked this one, too. The art of running down the clock ranks higher among many managers' coaching talents than the actual skills and tactics of the game itself. Take your time over goalkicks. 'Accidentally' drop the ball when trying to take a throw-in. Use all your substitutes but get the players to walk off. Whack the ball into Row Z.

The concept of injury-time was invented to make up for long stoppages when players needed treatment, but referees have now been given the power to add on time for any stoppage. Consequently, additional playing time of four minutes is not uncommon and sometimes as many as seven or eight are added on. In 1993 Manchester United benefited from seven added minutes to score two goals against Sheffield Wednesday for a 2-1 win that proved crucial to them winning the Premiership title. Ever since, manager Alex Ferguson has kept a careful eye on the time.

Right: Arsenal manager Tom Whittaker (left) and trainer Wally Milne show their anxiety during the closing minutes of a game in October, 1947

Far right: Manchester United manager Sir Alex Ferguson makes an obvious point of checking his watch as his team go down 2–0 to Liverpool in the Premiership in March, 2001

vodafone
vodafone

Shell-shocked

If you can meet with Triumph and Disaster
And treat those two imposters just the same...
...Yours is the Earth and everything that's in it
And – which is more – you'll be a Man, my son!

If, Rudyard Kipling

TRY TELLING THAT TO SOMEONE whose team has just lost a cup final to a last-minute goal. In the 1966 Greek Cup Final, the players of Pansseraikos were knocked flat by a last-minute goal that gave the cup to Olympiakos. The instant deflation, the inability to do anything but lie prostrate and hope the ground will swallow you up and take away your pain is there for all to see.

Thirty-three years later, the most eventful three minutes in the history of the European Cup left the players of Bayern Munich in an identical position on the turf of Barcelona's Nou Camp stadium. Leading Manchester United 1–0 with minutes to go, they conceded an equaliser on the stroke of full-time, scored by substitute Teddy Sheringham. Then, as everybody waited for the final whistle and extra time, Ole Gunnar Solskjaer stabbed the ball home for a late, late United winner. German players were seen beating the ground in dismay. For United, it capped a Treble of Premier League, FA Cup and European Cup.

Above: May 26, 1999, sees the most dramatic conclusion to a European Cup Final, as Manchester United's two late goals leave Jens Jeremies and his Bayern Munich colleagues in a state of collapse

Left: June 17, 1966, will forever be remembered as a black day by the fans of Greek club Pansseraikos, after they were shattered by a last-minute Olympiakos goal in the Greek Cup Final

1966

Overcome

WHO SAYS PLAYERS DON'T CARE? Twenty-four years apart, two World Cup tournaments reduced two of the great players of the age to tears. In 1966, when the World Cup was held in England, Portuguese striker Eusebio became the darling of the home fans.

With Pele effectively kicked out of the competition by brutal defenders, Eusebio took over the mantle of star player and helped to steer his side to the semi-finals – leading an extraordinary come-back against North Korea on the way. But the close attentions of England's Nobby Stiles finally nullified Eusebio's influence and England beat Portugal 2–1.

In 1990, Paul Gascoigne captured hearts at Italia 90 much as Eusebio had done in 1966. A booking picked up in the semi-final against Germany meant he would be ineligible for the final, should England get through. Gascoigne realised this immediately and was overcome with emotion. In the end, England lost the semi-final 4–3 on penalties, and Gazza bade a tearful farewell to the fans that he had won over with his imaginative, dynamic football. It was an historic moment, when football wore its heart on its sleeve and began to win back the family audience.

Left: July 4, 1990, and Paul Gascoigne breaks down in front of the England fans after losing to Germany on penalties in the World Cup semi-final in Turin

Far left: The great Portugal star Eusebio shows his bitter disappointment at being knocked out of the 1966 World Cup by England at Wembley on July 27

Sportsmanship

IT HAS BEEN SUGGESTED in some quarters that sportsmanship has all but disappeared from the game. There are plenty of matches in which this appears to be the case, but a glance through history shows that it was ever thus. Several World Cup matches in the early years of the tournament descended into mass brawls, often involving either Brazil or Argentina – these countries have accumulated the most red cards in World Cup Finals history. Meanwhile, England, often mocked as being too sporting for their own good, have developed their own hostile relationship with Argentina, dating back to their quarter-final meeting in the 1966 World Cup. Alf Ramsey was so incensed by the behaviour of the Argentines (who had their captain Rattin sent off), that he later likened them to 'animals'.

England's World Cup meetings with Argentina have been marred by controversy ever since. In 1986 Maradona scored with the famous Hand of God, and in 1998 David Beckham was sent off for reacting to a foul by Diego Simeone. But when the two players met again for their clubs less than a year later, there was a sporting handshake and an exchange of shirts that would have made Sir Alf's blood boil. Sportsmanship, it seems, survives all.

Above: March 3, 1999: David Beckham (right) shakes hands with Argentinean midfielder Diego Simeone after Manchester United's 2–0 Champions League win over Inter at Old Trafford. The previous time they had met, Beckham was sent off for England against Argentina at France 98

Left: Following the acrimonious World Cup quarter-final between England and Argentina on July 23, 1966, Alf Ramsey tries to stop his full-back George Cohen from swapping shirts

1938

England v Germany

THE FIRST MATCH BETWEEN ENGLAND AND GERMANY was an impromptu kickabout in No Man's Land during a Christmas cease-fire in the First World War, which England won 17–12. But the first official international between the two nations, a 3–3 draw in Berlin, didn't take place until 1930. Since then, it has always been a compelling fixture, bursting with controversy. The third official meeting was on May 14, 1938, again in Berlin, and by now Adolf Hitler was in charge. The England team were persuaded to give him the Nazi salute, much to their embarrassment, and they took it out on the German opposition, thrashing them 6–3.

England had the better of the results after that, even as Germany split into East and West, but saved the best for the World Cup final in 1966, winning 4–2 after extra time. Then came the drought. It would take another 34 years for England to beat Germany again in meaningful competition and another year before they won again on German soil. But it was worth waiting for. In a crucial World Cup qualifier, England recovered from going a goal behind to win 5–1. In no uncertain terms, the dam had burst.

LIST OF PHOTOGRAPHS: PAGE 2 England World Cup-winners (HULTON ARCHIVE) **Pp 6-7** Clough (B/W: HULTON ARCHIVE, colour: Jamie McDonald, GETTY IMAGES) **Pp 8-9** Stars of the show (HULTON ARCHIVE) **Pp 10-11** Training exercise (B/W: HULTON ARCHIVE, colour: Ross Kinnaird, GETTY IMAGES) **Pp 12-13** Physique (B/W: HULTON ARCHIVE, colour: GETTY IMAGES) **Pp 14-15** Training run (B/W: HULTON ARCHIVE, colour: Michael Steele, GETTY IMAGES) **Pp 16-17** Team photo (B/W: HULTON ARCHIVE, colour: Tom Shaw, GETTY IMAGES) **Pp 18-19** Get 'em young (B/W: HULTON ARCHIVE, colour: Dave Rogers, GETTY IMAGES) **Pp 20-21** The football family (B/W: HULTON ARCHIVE, colour: Alex Livesey, GETTY IMAGES) **Pp 22-23** Genius (B/W: HULTON ARCHIVE, colour: David Cannon, GETTY IMAGES) **Pp 24-25** The hero (B/W: HULTON ARCHIVE, colour: Clive Brunskill, GETTY IMAGES) **Pp 26-27** Star signing (B/W: HULTON ARCHIVE, colour: Ben Radford, GETTY IMAGES) **Pp 28-29** Icons (B/W: HULTON ARCHIVE, colour: Clive Mason, GETTY IMAGES) **Pp 30-31** Endorsements (B/W: HULTON ARCHIVE, colour: Clive Brunskill and Gary M. Prior, GETTY IMAGES) **Pp 32-33** Back home (B/W: HULTON ARCHIVE, colour: GETTY IMAGES) **Pp 34-35** A game of two halves (B/W: HULTON ARCHIVE, colour: GETTY IMAGES) **Pp 36-37** A little sunshine (B/W: HULTON ARCHIVE, colour: GETTY IMAGES) **Pp 38-39** Can she kick it? (B/W: HULTON ARCHIVE, colour: GETTY IMAGES) **Pp 40-41** The boss (B/W: HULTON ARCHIVE, colour: GETTY IMAGES) **Pp 42-43** The impossible job (B/W: HULTON ARCHIVE, colour: Mark Thompson, GETTY IMAGES) **Pp 44-45** It's a family affair (B/W: HULTON ARCHIVE, colour: Shaun Botterill, GETTY IMAGES) **Pp 46-47** Who's the daddy? (B/W: HULTON ARCHIVE, colour: Shaun Botterill, GETTY IMAGES) **Pp 48-49** The festive season (B/W: HULTON ARCHIVE, colour: Ben Radford, GETTY IMAGES) **Pp 50-51** Theatres of dreams (HULTON ARCHIVE) **Pp 52-53** The ground (B/W: HULTON ARCHIVE, colour: Stu Forster, GETTY IMAGES) **Pp 54-55** Let there be light (B/W: HULTON ARCHIVE, colour: Clive Brunskill, GETTY IMAGES) **Pp 56-57** Making a meal of it (B/W: HULTON ARCHIVE, colour: Shaun Botterill, GETTY IMAGES) **Pp 58-59** Getting a view (B/W: HULTON ARCHIVE, colour: Phil Cole, GETTY IMAGES) **Pp 60-61** Cup Final day (B/W: HULTON ARCHIVE, colour: Shaun Botterill, GETTY IMAGES) **Pp 62-63** The tunnel (B/W: HULTON ARCHIVE, colour: Mark Thompson, GETTY IMAGES) **Pp 64-65** Architectural art (B/W: HULTON ARCHIVE, colour: Shaun Botterill, GETTY IMAGES) **Pp 66-67** The San Siro (B/W: HULTON ARCHIVE, colour: Alex Livesey, GETTY IMAGES) **Pp 68-69** The Twin Towers (B/W: HULTON ARCHIVE, colour: Christopher Lee, GETTY IMAGES) **Pp 70-71** On the bench (B/W: HULTON ARCHIVE, colour: Shaun Botterill, GETTY IMAGES) **Pp 72-73** Bath time (B/W: HULTON ARCHIVE, colour: GETTY IMAGES) **Pp 74-75** Come all ye faithful (HULTON ARCHIVE) **Pp 76-77** Fanatics (B/W: HULTON ARCHIVE, colour: Ben Radford, GETTY IMAGES) **Pp 78-79** Sign here please (B/W: HULTON ARCHIVE, colour: Michael Steele, GETTY IMAGES) **Pp 80-81** Football train (B/W: HULTON ARCHIVE, colour: Laurence Griffiths, GETTY IMAGES) **Pp 82-83** Colours (B/W: HULTON ARCHIVE, colour: Ben Radford, GETTY IMAGES) **Pp 84-85** Vantage point (B/W: HULTON ARCHIVE, colour: GETTY IMAGES) **Pp 86-87** Celebrity fans (B/W: HULTON ARCHIVE, colour: Stu Forster, GETTY IMAGES) **Pp 88-89** Tartan army (B/W: HULTON ARCHIVE, colour: Shaun Botterill, GETTY IMAGES) **Pp 90-91** Young fans (B/W: HULTON ARCHIVE, colour: GETTY IMAGES) **Pp 92-93** Banter (B/W: HULTON ARCHIVE, colour: Shaun Botterill, GETTY IMAGES) **Pp 94-95** On the box (B/W: HULTON ARCHIVE, colour: GETTY IMAGES) **Pp 96-97** Street football (B/W: HULTON ARCHIVE, colour: GETTY IMAGES) **Pp 98-99** The power of the brand (B/W: HULTON ARCHIVE, colour: Clive Brunskill, GETTY IMAGES) **Pp 100-101** They also serve... (HULTON ARCHIVE) **PP 102-103** The draw (B/W: HULTON ARCHIVE, colour: Shaun Botterill, GETTY IMAGES) **Pp 104-105** Preparing the surface (B/W: HULTON ARCHIVE, colour: Stu Forster, GETTY IMAGES) **Pp 106-107** Programme seller (B/W: HULTON ARCHIVE, colour: GETTY IMAGES) **Pp 108-109** Good luck charm (B/W: HULTON ARCHIVE, colour: Mike Finn-Kelcey, GETTY IMAGES) **Pp 110-111** Mr chairman (B/W: HULTON ARCHIVE, colour: GETTY IMAGES) **Pp 112-113** Razzmatazz (B/W: HULTON ARCHIVE, colour: GETTY IMAGES) **Pp 114-115** Police presence (B/W: HULTON ARCHIVE, colour: GETTY IMAGES) **Pp 116-117** Keeping the peace (B/W: HULTON ARCHIVE, colour: Shaun Botterill GETTY IMAGES) **Pp 118-119** The man in er... (B/W: HULTON ARCHIVE, colour: Alex Livesey GETTY IMAGES) **Pp 120-121** On camera (B/W: HULTON ARCHIVE, colour: Ben Radford GETTY IMAGES) **Pp 122-123** Authority figure (B/W: HULTON ARCHIVE, colour: Clive Brunskill, GETTY IMAGES) **Pp 124-125** The magic sponge (B/W: HULTON ARCHIVE, colour: Ross Kinnaird, GETTY IMAGES) **Pp 126-127** Press box (B/W: HULTON ARCHIVE, colour: Shaun Botterill, GETTY IMAGES) **Pp 128-129** Media pressure (B/W: HULTON ARCHIVE, colour: Laurence Griffiths, GETTY IMAGES) **Pp 130-131** Objects of desire (HULTON ARCHIVE) **Pp 132-133** The object of the exercise (B/W: HULTON ARCHIVE, colour: Ross Kinnaird, GETTY IMAGES) **Pp 134-135** These colours don't run (B/W: HULTON ARCHIVE, colour: Ben Radford, GETTY IMAGES) **Pp 136-137** Shirt numbers (B/W: HULTON ARCHIVE, colour: Shaun Botterill, GETTY IMAGES) **Pp 138-139** Footwear (B/W: HULTON ARCHIVE, colour: Stu Forster, GETTY IMAGES) **Pp 140-141** Getting the message across (B/W: HULTON ARCHIVE, colour: Craig Prentis, GETTY IMAGES) **Pp 142-143** Card play (B/W: HULTON ARCHIVE, colour: David Cannon, GETTY IMAGES) **Pp 144-145** The wall (B/W: HULTON ARCHIVE, colour: Laurence Griffiths, GETTY IMAGES) **Pp 146-147** Refreshment (B/W: HULTON ARCHIVE, colour: David Cannon, GETTY IMAGES) **Pp 148-149** Carried off (B/W: HULTON ARCHIVE, colour: Phil Cole, GETTY IMAGES) **Pp 150-151** Time piece (B/W: HULTON ARCHIVE, colour: Ben Radford, GETTY IMAGES) **Pp 152-153** What's the score? (B/W: HULTON ARCHIVE, colour: GETTY IMAGES) **Pp 154-155** Chariots of fire (B/W: HULTON ARCHIVE, colour: GETTY IMAGES) **Pp 156-157** When the whistle blows (HULTON ARCHIVE) **Pp 158-159** Fly-past (B/W: HULTON ARCHIVE, colour: Gary M.Prior, GETTY IMAGES) **Pp 160-161** Goalkick (B/W: HULTON ARCHIVE, colour: David Cannon, GETTY IMAGES) **Pp 162-163** Aerial combat (B/W: HULTON ARCHIVE, colour: Clive Brunskill, GETTY IMAGES) **Pp 164-165** Putting yourself about (B/W: HULTON ARCHIVE, colour: Shaun Botterill, GETTY IMAGES) **Pp 166-167** Never the twain (B/W: HULTON ARCHIVE, colour: Clive Brunskill, GETTY IMAGES) **Pp 168-169** Flying save (B/W: HULTON ARCHIVE, colour: GETTY IMAGES) **Pp 170-171** Handbags (B/W: HULTON ARCHIVE, colour: Alex Livesey, GETTY IMAGES) **Pp 172-173** It never rains (B/W: HULTON ARCHIVE, colour: Laurence Griffiths, GETTY IMAGES) **Pp 174-175** Yeeeeeeeees! (B/W: HULTON ARCHIVE, colour: Ben Radford, GETTY IMAGES) **Pp 176-177** That sinking feeling (B/W: HULTON ARCHIVE, colour: David Cannon, GETTY IMAGES) **Pp 178-179** In the net (B/W: HULTON ARCHIVE, colour: Mark Thompson, GETTY IMAGES) **Pp 180-181** How long to go? (B/W: HULTON ARCHIVE, colour: Michael Steele, GETTY IMAGES) **Pp 182-183** Shell-shocked (B/W: HULTON ARCHIVE, colour: Shaun Botterill, GETTY IMAGES) **Pp 184-185** Overcome (B/W: HULTON ARCHIVE, colour: David Cannon, GETTY IMAGES) **Pp 186-187** Sportsmanship (B/W: HULTON ARCHIVE, colour: Ben Radford, GETTY IMAGES) **Pp 188-189** England v Germany (B/W: HULTON ARCHIVE, colour: Ben Radford, GETTY IMAGES) **Pp 190-191** The cup that cheers (B/W: HULTON ARCHIVE, colour: Stu Forster, GETTY IMAGES)

Thanks to Lee Martin and Richard Pitts at Getty Images along with Mark Trowbridge whose help in picture research for this book went beyond the call of duty. Thanks too to Pat Murphy and Brian Clough.

The cup that cheers

WE'VE SPOKEN ABOUT THE CHANGING attitudes towards liquid refreshment, but these pictures bring the matter into even clearer focus. They also tell a story in their own right. Brazil is famous for the coffee it produces but who would have thought they used to drink it at half-time? This picture was taken in 1955 and, as the record books show, Brazil went on to win three of the next four World Cups, playing in such a laid-back style that we can only assume they'd given up the half-time coffee by 1958.

Today, dieticians will give you scientific reasons why coffee and tea aren't the revitalising drinks they were once considered to be. The same goes for alcohol, although that message is much more serious. Paul Merson and Paul Gascoigne are just two examples of the many footballers that have become dependent on alcohol and have sought medical help. Today the help is there and it is not out of place to celebrate promotion with a soft drink. But in years gone by, the alcoholic in the dressing room would have gone unnoticed, or at least uncared for, until it was too late.

Right: The Brazil team in 1955 show faith in their country's national product by enjoying a nice cup of coffee during the half-time interval

Far right: Paul Merson (left) and Paul Gascoigne of Middlesbrough celebrate their 4–1 win over Oxford United in May 1998 to take Boro back into the top flight

Above: England's finest hour against Germany since 1966, and their first win away since 1965, is marked on the scoreboard in Munich's Olympic Stadium on September 1, 2001

Left: May 14, 1938, with war just around the corner, England line up against Germany in Berlin to salute Adolf Hitler before going on to win 6–3